MILLION DOLLAR COACH

TAKI MOORE

MILLION DOLLAR COACH

TAKI MOORE

Copyright © 2016 Coach Marketing Services Pty Ltd

All rights reserved. No part of this book may be used or reproduced in any manner whatsoever without prior written consent of the authors, except as provided by the Australian and United States of America copyright law.

Published by More Clients®, Newport Beach, NSW, Australia

Printed in the United States of America.

ISBN-13: 978-1539941675
ISBN-10: 1539941671

This publication is designed to provide accurate and authoritative information with regard to the subject matter covered. It is sold with the understanding that the publisher is not engaged in rendering legal, accounting, or other professional advice. If legal advice or other expert assistance is required, the services of a competent professional should be sought. The opinions expressed by the authors in this book are not endorsed by Best Seller Publishing® and are the sole responsibility of the author rendering the opinion.

Most Million Dollar Coach and Coach Marketing Services titles are available at special quantity discounts for bulk purchases for sales promotions, premiums, fundraising, and educational use. Special versions or book excerpts can also be created to fit specific needs.

For more information, please write to:

Coach Marketing Services

PO Box 489

Five Dock NSW 2049

Australia

Visit us online at: www.MillionDollarCoach.com

Dedication

For Ethan, and living in summer.

Epigraph

I firmly believe that any man's finest hour, the greatest fulfilment of all that he holds dear, is that moment when he has worked his heart out for a good cause and lies exhausted on the field of battle - victorious.

— Vince Lombardi

Preface

Back in late 2008, early 2009, I started a consulting business for small companies with one of my best mates, Mike. I'd left the coaching company that I worked for as marketing manager, and we were out doing our own thing, helping people with their marketing.

I'd get the deal and sign up the client. Together, he and I would create the strategy. I did most of the copywriting, he'd create the design, and we'd ship stuff to clients. We were good at it. Within four months, we were completely booked out. There was no more time available. We were working hard for clients. We developed a waitlist. The problem was that we had too much work and not nearly enough money. I had five kids, and so did he.

We decided to go our separate ways and split the clients down the middle. I worked with the coaches, and Mike looked after the other clients. Now I was on my own and fully booked. At the time, I was thinking about moving to something leveraged because I was doing one-on-one consulting and coaching. I had an idea about how it would work, that it would be less expensive than my one-on-one, but I'd make it up on volume.

I wanted the flexible time that a leveraged coaching practice would give me, but not just for fun (although I love fun!). The main reason why I wanted to change my business was my son Ethan. My son has epilepsy, autism, and cerebral palsy. But he's also hilariously funny, quick-witted, and very smart. Because of his health challenges, every now and again, he has to go in for a big operation. Every time we go, something seems to go wrong, and his care becomes all-consuming.

Have you ever been in a hospital ward, with someone you love hooked up to the machine that goes *bing*? There's a "beep-beep" that tracks the oxygen saturation in the patient's blood, and then it drops? That's terrifying. You hit the big red button, and the crash team runs in to resuscitate him. Oh man, you take one step back looking at your son, who's there in the bed. You hold your wife's hand, hope, and pray. These experiences had made me realise I wanted to turn to a leveraged coaching practice, but I hadn't decided on the specifics yet.

The pivotal moment happened when I came home one day, and my wife said, "Hey, Hon, I have some news."

I sat down. She looked at me and held my hand.

"I'm pregnant."

I felt completely conflicted. I was thrilled to bits, of course, but inside I was freaking out because we were not doing well financially. I had just borrowed 200 bucks from my friend Sam to buy food that week.

"Oh, man."

The news came at a busy time. Ethan was enrolled in a private school at $25,000 a year, and I wasn't making nearly enough to meet expenses. Our son needed lots of support, and we had four other kids, too. And in the middle of that whirlwind, I got this news: We will soon have another mouth to feed. That's what got me to launch this thing.

I configured my business in such a way that if I need to step away for a while, I can. I take care of my family, and the business continues without me.

I wrote this book because there are so many great coaches with knowledge and skills who can help others. Either they don't have enough clients, or they are overbooked and have no time to enjoy life. The goal is to help you get the right type of clients and scale up so you have plenty of free time. Let's build the business that lets you spend more time with people you love.

I had 200 bucks in the bank when I started this business. It was my friend Sam who once asked me, "How would you feel about having a million-dollar-a-year tax bill?"

I said, "Mate, I don't want to pay that much tax."

He said, "You're missing the point. If you had to pay a million dollars a year in taxes, think about how much money you'd be earning."

I realised, "Oh."

Taki Moore

My name is Taki Moore. I'm going to teach you how to attract, convert, deliver, and scale a coaching business. This book, Million Dollar Coach, reveals the nine strategies that drive a seven-figure coaching business.

There are plenty of coaches out there in the startup phase of their business. Maybe they earn up to $5,000 a month at first, and they're barely making a living. I call that survival. They will always peak at a certain level because they're spread too thin, and their marketing is ineffective. They don't have enough leads, appointments, clients, or money. My job is to help them launch and double their earnings quickly. If that's what you need, pay close attention; this book will be very helpful for you.

The second thing I do (which occupies about 90% of my time) is help coaches scale their business. This group, enrolled in the Black Belt program, is already earning $10,000 a month or more. My job is to help them scale their business and give them three things: more money, more meaning (they get the satisfaction of helping others), and more freedom. I help them create a business that is the basis for a wonderful, liberated, free life.

> I don't know where you're at right now. I'd love to know what you need most. Do you need to launch because you're not at $10,000 a month yet? Or do you need to scale?

Worksheets

My goal is to create the world's best book for coaches on how to grow and scale their businesses. This book is packed full of the strategies and tools I used to take my business over $1,000,000 a year — the same strategies, tools, and worksheets I use with clients in my Black Belt program.

You can download them all from www.MillionDollarCoach.com/kit. Jump on the link, download the kit, and get ready to get busy.

Keep your worksheets handy and complete them as you read the book.

Table of Contents

INTRODUCTION: The Million Dollar Coach 15

    THE MODEL: ATTRACT/CONVERT/DELIVER 15

Part One: Attract... 23

    STRATEGY 1:   Fill Your Funnel... 25

    STRATEGY 2:   Build Authority... 45

    STRATEGY 3:   Install Automation.. 61

Part Two: Convert 71

    STRATEGY 4:   Audition Clients 73

    STRATEGY 5:   Rock Event 97

    STRATEGY 6:   Sell Webinars..117

Part Three: Deliver 131

    STRATEGY 7:   Decide Model 133

    STRATEGY 8:   Unpack IP 151

    STRATEGY 9:   Leverage Talent 171

    SUMMARY: THE MILLION DOLLAR PATH 185

Introduction

Every coaching business is built on three pillars: how to attract leads and prospects, how to convert those prospects into clients, and how to deliver your products and services.

Attract is how we generate the leads, online and off, and then how we warm them up to the point where they're an 8, 9, or 10 in terms of how likely they are to give you money and sign up as a client. That's what we talk about in the first part of this book.

Convert is how we convert prospects into clients, how we go from cold to sold, or curious to committed. In the second part, I'll show you everything I've learned about auditioning clients one on one, rocking live events, and selling on webinars.

Deliver is all about how we design and deliver a coaching program that frees you up from one-on-one, time-for-money work. In this part, we're going to decide the coaching model that you're going to build. We're going to unpack your IP, the knowledge in your head, and turn it into a system that a client or a group of clients can follow. Then we're going to leverage the talent of a small team to set you up so you can get more done and focus on the stuff that you're great at.

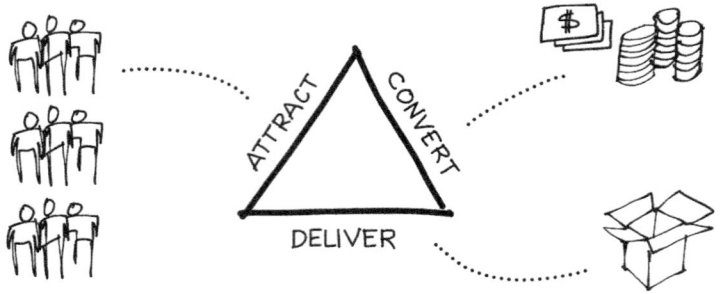

ATTRACT, CONVERT, DELIVER: THE 3 PILLARS OF EVERY COACHING BUSINESS.

You can do okay by winging it, but hitting a million dollars — certainly in my case — took some serious focus on these three core parts of my coaching business.

Think about the way that most coaches attract, convert, and deliver: They do it manually. They cold-call. They knock on doors. They go to networking events, and they collect cards, chase, and follow up. Then they convert — onesie-twosie. That is, they have a conversation for maybe an hour with a potential client, in the hope that the potential client says yes. Often they say no, and they give you objections, excuses, and stalls.

COACHING BUSINESS 1.0–MANUAL, ONESIE-TWOSIE, TIME FOR MONEY.

The whole process is drawn out, it takes longer than necessary, and at the end of the hour, maybe you get a client — but often you don't. It's frustrating. You might have the best script in the world, but the prospect doesn't have the script, and they certainly don't follow it.

The way most coaches deliver is time-for-money. We do an hour a week, or an hour every two weeks, whatever it is for you. We have scheduled conversations with clients. It's time-for-money, so there is no way to get free. Eventually, you hit a ceiling: There is no more money you can make, because there are no more hours in your day.

If you think about these three activities, manual prospecting, selling onesie-twosie, and delivering time-for-money, then what's the common element? You are. You're in the middle of all of them. There is only so much time available; you have only a finite amount of energy; 81% of coaches burn out after three years because of that model. It's not your fault; it's how the other guys taught you to do stuff. This isn't the solution to our problems. It's the very thing killing us.

My Discovery

I figured out that instead of manually chasing prospects, I could automate my marketing with online lead generation, bringing all the leads I need every day, every week, every month. This process warms people up to the point where, on that scale from one to ten (regarding how likely they are to give me money), the warmest are the 8s, 9s, and 10s, who are ready to talk to us about joining our program.

In terms of converting, instead of selling onesie-twosie, I figured out how to sell one-to-many. I have webinars and events around the perfect pipeline. Indoctrination events, funnel filters, Triage Calls and the strategy sessions for starting are big and expensive. Then all processes and leverage are scalable.

With delivery, instead of time-for-money coaching, I figured out how to build a leveraged coaching program that lets me help hundreds or thousands of people instead of a dozen. With leveraged programs, I can help way more people and maximise my impact, while getting them the same kind of results that they'd get if they were with me one-on-one.

This gave me all the money I could want and more, plus it's given us a ton of freedom. We have four months off a year, travelling all around the world, having a blast with our kids and our friends.

I call it Coaching Business 2.0 because it's not built around time and effort anymore. Coaching Business 2.0 is built on Systems and IP, and creates money, meaning, and freedom.

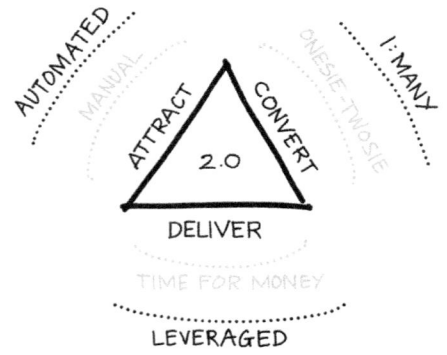

COACHING BUSINESS 2.0—AUTOMATED, 1: MANY, LEVERAGED.

There are nine strategies that I use in my own business, and that I teach my Black Belt clients. These strategies help us generate leads, convert prospects into clients, and deliver leveraged coaching programs. That way, I can help hundreds or thousands of people all over the world achieve the same kind of results I'd get if we were working together one-on-one.

These are the nine strategies that drive a seven-figure coaching business.

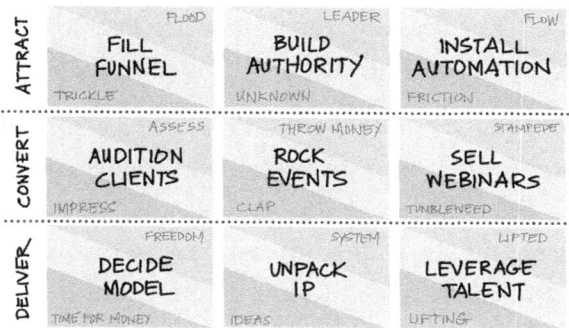

9 STRATEGIES THAT DRIVE A MILLION DOLLAR COACHING BUSINESS.

In Part One, we'll look at the first three strategies that make up the Attract pillar of your business. In Strategy 1, I'll show you how to turn a trickle of leads into a flood and a dried-up sales pipeline into all the leads you need. Every day, when you wake up and check your inbox, it will be full of another 10, 20, or 50 leads who are already warmed up and ready to take the next step with you.

In Strategy 2, we build authority. I'll show you how to position yourself in a way that takes you from being unknown in your marketplace to becoming the prominent expert, a trusted advisor, the person your prospects turn to for advice. What do most people do when the marketplace is noisier than ever, they're unknown, and their prospects are sceptical? They try to shout louder. The secret is not to shout at all, but to whisper the right words in the right ear at the right time. I'll show you how it's done with authority marketing.

In Strategy 3, I'll show you how to install automation in your business so you can eliminate the friction that stops you from being as consistent as you need to be. Installing automation takes you from friction to flow, so you can build a system once, and never have to worry about dropping the ball. Automation gives you the freedom to focus on the things you do best.

In Part Two, we'll deep dive into three strategies that help you convert prospects into clients more quickly, easily, and effectively than ever.

In Strategy 4, I'll show you how to audition clients so that, instead of working hard to impress your prospects, you create a situation where you're assessing them. When you remember that they're the ones with the problem and you're the one with the solution, every sales appointment can be like an audition on American Idol, where you're Simon Cowell in the judge's seat. Auditioning clients flips the power dynamic in your favour.

In Strategy 5 and 6, I'll show you how to use live events and webinars to convert whole groups of prospects at once. Many coaches and consultants struggle to convert prospects at live events because they focus on teaching, and then they try to tack a sale onto the back of their presentation. People love the content, but they don't buy. I'll show you how to build the sale into your events and webinars so that, at the end, you'll have prospects handing you order forms, not feedback forms.

Part Three focuses on the delivery side of your coaching business: building leveraged coaching programs that deliver the results your clients need and give you the freedom to expand your business, or just goof off and have a great time with the people you love.

In Strategy 7, we'll decide which business model will work best for you; whether to start with a shorter six-week program, or go for a longer 12-month deal. Either way, you'll end up with a business that frees you up from time-for-money coaching and delivers the kind of freedom you need to scale your business up to the next level.

In Strategy 8, I'll show you how to unpack your intellectual property so you can take all the information and ideas in your head and the solutions you're already helping clients with, and turn them into a Signature System. When you use Signature Systems for coaching, you lead your clients to results, rather than reacting and responding to each of them one by one.

In Strategy 9, I'll show you how to leverage the talents of others so that, instead of lifting everyone up all the time, you have a team of people around you who can do the heavy lifting for you.

When you're trying to do everything on your own, you become the major bottleneck in your business. It's exhausting. Eventually, you'll drop the ball, decide it's all too hard or, worse, lower your expectations. I'll show you cost-effective ways to build a virtual team that lightens your workload.

Then, in the Summary, we *land the plane*. I'll show you how to put together a street-wise plan for implementing everything you've learned, a plan that gets you focused on what you have to do next – today, right now – to make a seven-figure coaching business a reality for you, the same way it became real for me.

You will notice that I have added conversations I have had with coaching clients on my webinars. In those paragraphs, my clients and I discuss the techniques I teach, as well as their main concerns, issues, hopes, and dreams with regards to their businesses. I wanted to share these conversations with you because they may inspire you or make you think twice about your own situation, but also because they are the perfect illustration of the new way I want you to approach your business.

Ready? Let's get into it…

PART ONE

ATTRACT

Chapter 1: Fill Funnel

There's nothing worse than wanting to throw an event and having 20 people on your invitation list. Maybe you've got thousands of people on your list, but they're just not responding the way you'd like. If your list is too small, or your response rates are too low, everything becomes harder. Small lists and low response rates limit the amount of money you can make, reduce the number of people you can help, and ultimately restrict the kind of freedom you can have.

On the other hand, when you have a big list, things are really different. List size is a multiplier. If you think about the formula for marketing effectiveness, it goes like this:

Marketing x List Size = Results

Let's assume you and I are equally talented at marketing. If you've got a big list, and I've got a small list, and we send the same email, we'll get the same response rates, right? But because of the different list sizes, you're going to get a result that's 20, 30, or 100 times better than mine, just because your list was bigger. A big list buys you better results.

A big list buys you speed. You can ramp up quickly because all you have to do is send the message. To write this book, for example, I sent one email saying, "Hi, I've been stuck in writing my book. I'd really love some help." One email, and 658 people registered for my book-writing webinar. Why? Because list size is a multiplier. If I'd had 100 or 200 people on my list that would never have happened.

By the way, a big list makes you way more attractive to potential joint venture partners, too. A great friend of mine, Bill, asked me, "Who do you think I should partner with in Australia?" I said, "What's your idea of an ideal partner?" The first thing he said was, "At least 25,000 subscribers or more." You make a way more attractive partner with a list of 25,000 subscribers.

A big list also covers up a bunch of imperfections. You don't have to be as good when you're bigger. I make screw-ups all the time, but the list is growing every single day, so what happens? Well, we still do really well because the list size covers many of those mistakes.

Once, I accidentally sent a blank email to my whole database with nothing but an unsubscribe link, no content at all, not even "Hi, First name". Just the unsubscribe link. Brilliant. I sent out a follow-up note, and we wound up signing seven or eight brand new clients as a direct result of recovering from my screw-up.

> So list size is a multiplier: It improves results, buys you speed, and covers a bunch of imperfections. The question I've got for you right now is this: Why do you want to grow your list? *More opportunities to sell. I can impact more people, reach more potential sales, create more leads, save more people.* Exactly, more people, more impact. *Been marketing to the same people for the last eight years. I want to help and reach more people with my message. Get better results.* Yeah. *Need more great clients,* says Eric. All of the things you just mentioned, Jerry. Perfect, so I did a good job. Time to leverage a brand new game, yes. *I need to grow my business. I've got great products, but a small list.* Exactly.

When it comes to building your list, there are two key elements at work. First, there's traffic. Traffic is the online marketing word for visitors to your website — you want as much of it as you can get. Second, we need conversion. If all we have is traffic, but we do a bad job converting, nothing good happens. People visit once, then disappear forever. Traffic first, then conversions, okay?

Here are three key principles that will help you get the leads you need to grow your list: select your source, offer a gateway drug, and work the money map.

Select Your Source

Selecting your source is just like choosing the channel on your TV. There are three core channels you can choose from to generate leads for your coaching business. Only three; not 10, not 100. It might look like there are a hundred different ways, especially online, since there are new marketing tools every week. But really, there are just three ways to generate the leads you need. Together, we're going to choose which one is best for you.

You can do free marketing, paid marketing, or partnership marketing.

Free Marketing

Content marketing is free, but it's really about authority. It's identifying who your perfect prospect is, creating great content for them, putting that content up on your website, syndicating it around the world, and then bringing those people back to your website to sign them up.

My friend, Jess Ranker, says your website is like the head of an octopus. That's where the content lives, where the opt-ins are, where your opportunity to collect leads lives. The octopus's tentacles spread out across hot traffic sites on the web: YouTube, iTunes, Google, Facebook, Twitter, LinkedIn, Pinterest, Periscope — whatever is popular with your people.

Free marketing is all about creating great content and sharing it all over the internet. It's an awesome strategy, it's a core part of my business, and it's a core part of my clients' businesses. It's great because it positions you as the authority in your field. The downside is that it's slow. It takes a while to build up the content, and to gain the traction you're after.

Content marketing is awesome, but it's not instant.

Paid Marketing

Step Two is working out how you'll attract them. How are you going to get them to your website, then entice them to swap their email address for something cool?

Step Three is building a mechanism for taking that email address and turning it into a client.

Paid marketing is beautiful because it's so fast and completely measurable. With paid marketing, you can create a lead magnet in the morning, put an ad up in the afternoon, and see leads coming in overnight or the next morning. You can tell right away which messages work and which don't.

Paid marketing is one of my favourite go-to strategies. If you want to build a list quickly, paid is where it's at.

Partnership Marketing

The third strategy is partnership marketing: identifying other people who already have the audience that you want and building a business relationship with them.

They've already spent thousands — possibly tens, or even hundreds, of thousands of dollars and countless hours — building relationships with their prospects and customers, the same people you'd like to reach.

They already have the trust that you need, so we want to engineer a "trust transfer". The easiest way to do that is to get them to introduce you. Because they're introducing you, some of their love and trust rubs off on you, and all of a sudden you're loved and trusted as well.

For the first three years of my business, all I did was partnership marketing.

They're called joint ventures or partnerships, sometimes they're affiliate deals. For me, it was less about marketing strategy and more about personality style. I'm a natural connector. I find it really easy to talk to people and work out a win-win for both of us. If you're a good people person, partnerships could be great for you, too. (If you're not really a people person, stay away from partnerships. Go with paid instead.)

The three core steps to partnership marketing are: *Identify*, *Approach*, and *Serve and Strategise*.

Step One: Identify your perfect partners. There's usually a category (or categories) of business that could refer you. You want to identify the individuals, the principals in those businesses.

Step Two: Approach. We usually send a couple of short emails to get you an appointment with the right people.

Step Three: We serve and strategise. We give potential partners all the help we can and then, in the last 20 minutes of the appointment, we strategise a way that we could work together and have them introduce you to their database.

When marketing legend, Jay Abraham, was asked, "If we could just take away every single strategy you know, and you have to start from scratch with no money, no list, no nothing, and you can pick one strategy and bring it with you, what would that be?" Jay said, "Partnership and endorsed marketing, without a doubt."

So, to sum up, content marketing is amazing. It positions you as the expert, but it takes a while to build. Paid marketing is instant. You can turn it on whenever you want, but it's going to cost a little bit of money to get started. Partnership marketing is fantastic when you're starting out with very little money and no list of your own.

Once we've selected our source — once we've chosen how we're going to get our message out to people — we have to entice them into our world. The best way to do that is to offer them a 'gateway drug.'

www.MillionDollarCoach.com/kit

Offer a Gateway Drug

What we mean, of course, is that we offer them a first step that makes them think, "That looks fantastic, I love it, I want more."

Now, most coaches and consultants offer something like a free sales appointment, which, when you think about it, isn't all that attractive for a prospect. Or they offer a free newsletter, which isn't really all that sexy either. Sometimes they make a real effort and put together a video course, which could be super high value for prospects, but it's a bit of a pain, both to create and to watch because it takes a real time commitment.

When you're planning your first step with prospects, there are two core factors to think about: risk and reward. Obviously, we want something that's high reward; in other words, something that's going to be really useful and valuable.

Whether somebody responds or not comes down to whether they think the reward outweighs the risk of engaging. It's like a see-saw. If one end is heavy on the reward, we're more likely to tip that way and respond.

On the other hand, if the other end of the see-saw is heavy on the risk, we'll tip that way and won't respond at all. Risk could be anything from having to talk to a pushy sales person, to filling out a nine-page questionnaire, or even watching hours' worth of video with no guarantee it'll help. All those things are annoying, and if they're more hassle than the reward is worth, your prospect will walk away.

So we want to create an offer that's as high reward as possible and as low risk as possible.

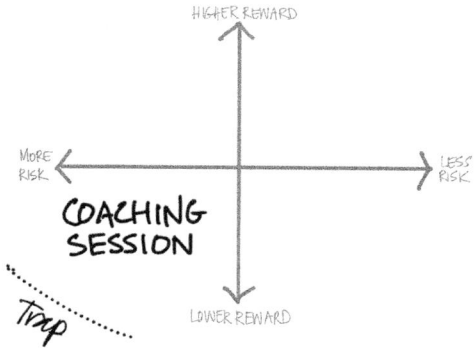

OFFER A GATEWAY DRUG - ONE THATS HIGH REWARD, LOW RISK.

Now, "free coaching session" is really just code for "sales appointment", at least from the prospect's point of view. They think the only reason you're coming to see them is to sell them stuff, to talk them into buying from you, and that it's going to waste a lot of their time. That's a bit scary for a prospect. It's high risk and low reward. It's a trap.

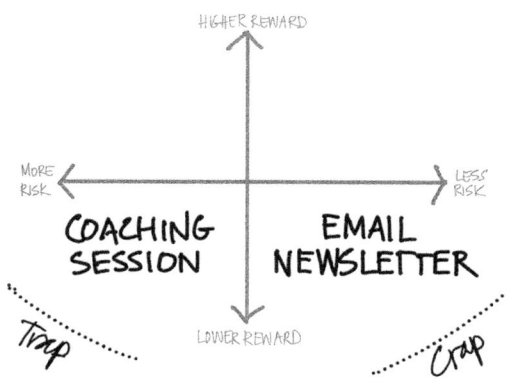

OFFER A GATEWAY DRUG - ONE THATS HIGH REWARD, LOW RISK.

Free newsletters are okay, and they're pretty low risk from the prospect's perspective. But who really needs more email newsletters in their inbox? They're low risk, but they're low reward too, just more crap you could do without.

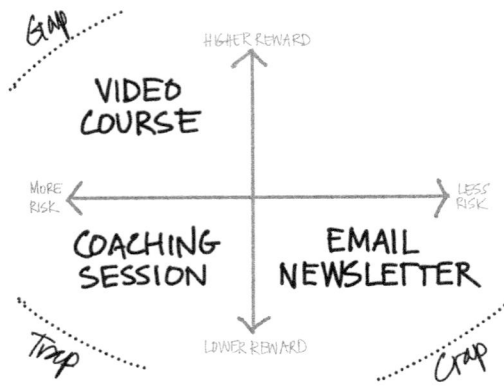

OFFER A GATEWAY DRUG – ONE THATS HIGH REWARD, LOW RISK.

Some people make more of an effort and build something like a free video course with really great content as a kind of sample of what to expect. The reward is high, but so is the risk — both for you (because it takes time and effort to create the content) and for them (because it takes time and commitment to watch and participate). It's potentially high reward, but it's definitely high risk because of the hassle factor. There's a bit of a gap between the amount of risk (effort) and the potential reward.

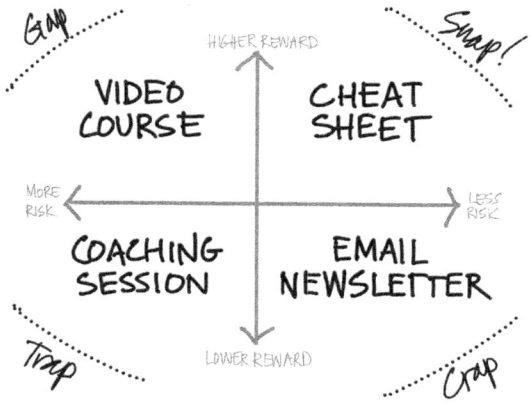

OFFER A GATEWAY DRUG — ONE THATS HIGH REWARD, LOW RISK.

The best lead magnet I've ever created — by miles — is a cheat sheet, a short guide, or a downloadable PDF, because it's really useful for the prospect and was really low hustle for me. In fact, I already had all the content, I just repackaged it into a short guide: two, three, four pages, something quick and easy.

When you're building a lead magnet, you want to follow a few simple rules. Just think "SAGE":

- Short
- Actionable
- Goal-oriented
- Easy

First, it has to be short – short enough to be consumed in something like four to seven minutes.

It has to be actionable, loaded up with practical, useful content, in a fill-in-the-blanks or step-by-step format.

It has to be goal-oriented. If you think about it, your prospects are in a particular situation with a particular problem and want to hear how they can get a particular kind of outcome. That's the goal. Be super clear about what you're going to work on together and even clearer about the results that work will get them.

And finally, this first step has to be easy — easy enough for a beginner to take with confidence.

(If you'd like to see an example, you can check out The Triage Call lead magnet on my website.)

Work the Money Map

There's a specific process we follow for building marketing funnels with our clients. It goes something like this: Lead Magnet - Channel - Conversion Tool - Follow-up Funnel.

Your prospects see you through your chosen channel, they download your lead magnet (in return for their email address), you follow up with your conversion tools — a one-on-one appointment, a webinar, or a live event (more on those in the next section), and then they buy your product or your service.

That's how it happens in a perfect world, but the world's not always perfect, right? People drop out of the funnel in all sorts of places, so we need a series of follow-up messages, emails, or videos to get people to come back and buy in again.

That's what we call working the money map.

Let's just quickly pause and check in.

Which of those has been most valuable so far? We talked about selecting your source, figuring out whether it's going to be free, paid, or a partnership. We also mentioned offering a gateway drug, something short, actionable, goal-oriented, and easy enough for beginners. Furthermore, we talked about working the money map, having a clear path from the channel, the lead magnet, the conversion tool, and the follow-up funnel. What has been the most helpful for you so far?

How do you syndicate content? I will talk about that in our next section. Paid traffic is scalable, yes. *Resource guide or cheat sheet*, says Paul, yes. *How do I know which source to select?* The short answer is: Figure out where your clients already are and go there. Any of them can work with almost every client. If you have a more corporate audience, then often, LinkedIn is going to be a way. Their placements are paid on LinkedIn or a partnership through another organisation database you want.

SAGE: Short, Actionable, Goal-oriented and Easy enough for a beginner. The money map, gateway drug. Perfect. Lots of people loving SAGE. *Instant down my gateway drug, easy to digest.* Yes, short, snappy, magnet, yeah. The best lead magnet that I have ever built, in terms of content pay, was a four-part video tube. Go to the top of my website. It says, "How to Attract, Convert & Deliver like a Million Dollar Coach" for the video. It's amazing, so proud of it. People that are in it love it, but it's just to consume my Triage Call seven-page PDF that people can get in and out quickly, get an instant result. They love that better. It converts at least twice as well.

This is Laurence.

This is Laurence, a great client of mine. When I first met him, he had 164 people in his database. Now he teaches chiropractors how to grow their businesses and reach more people. His core marketing strategy is free authority marketing by means of a weekly video blog.

When he started two years ago, Laurence was a full-time chiropractor. He wasn't even coaching, and he had just 164 people on his list. At his last event, a summit, he had over 700 customers paying to hear him and a line-up of speakers. As well as the summit, Laurence has a really great, leveraged coaching program. It was all built on authority marketing. We started off with nothing. We did email marketing into webinars, webinars into a six-week course, a six-week course into an event, and an event into a program, and now Laurence is absolutely melting it.

This is Rob. I love Rob; he's the reason I'm writing this book. Rob's business is helping people write, promote, and distribute books. His core marketing strategy is paid. He runs Facebook ads to a 17-minute case study video, at the end of which people can click a button to fill in a little form and book in for a triage call with Rob or one of his team.

When I met Rob, he was generating leads but not converting consistently well. We tweaked his marketing and his sales. Now he's absolutely smashing it, running a really good, million-dollar coaching business, all driven through paid Facebook traffic: from a case study, into a strategy session, into a client.

This is Howard.

This is Howard. He helps restaurants to market themselves. His core marketing strategy is partnership. He finds people who have relationships with the restaurants that he wants, does a partnership program with them, and has them invite their people along. Howard gives them a copy of his book (which establishes authority). Rob invites people to a webinar or an event where he converts them into his program.

> The question I've got for you is this: free, paid, or partnership — what's it going to be for you?
>
> I want you to just take 20 seconds right now to decide. Am I going to do free or paid, or partnership? What's it going to be? One of the things we need to talk about at one stage, is how good your current rate is. We're going to talk about that in our next chapter.
>
> Cassie says, *I'd love to learn more about how to approach people for a partnership.* Great, three steps. First, identify categories, what kinds of businesses would be a great match, and the specific partners,

who specifically would fit. All of this is like 12 people to talk to, to start this off.

Next, you approach them. You send a short email, like "Hey, Cassie, we haven't met yet, but I noticed that we both work with coaches [in a complementary, non-competitive kind of way]. I'd love to get to know you a little bit and see if there's any way that I can help you out. Would you be up for a quick chat some time? I'd love to help." People are generally happy to chat, and your job then is to find out some way to genuinely help each other out.

Funnel Tools

The two tools we use are the List-Building Essentials Worksheet and the Money Map.

List-Building Essentials

Worksheet...

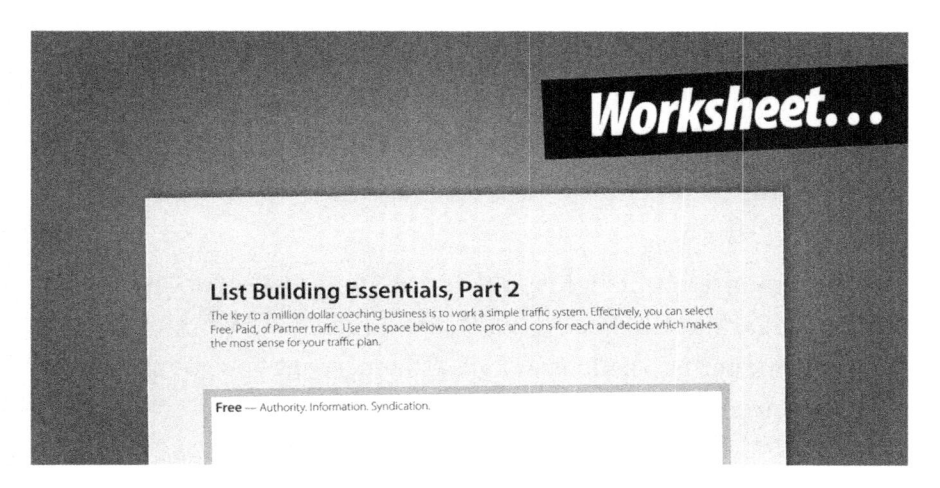

List Building Essentials, Part 2
The key to a million dollar coaching business is to work a simple traffic system. Effectively, you can select Free, Paid, or Partner traffic. Use the space below to note pros and cons for each and decide which makes the most sense for your traffic plan.

Free — Authority. Information. Syndication.

The **List-Building Essentials** worksheet walks you through free, paid, and partnership options and helps you decide which one you need.

The Money Map

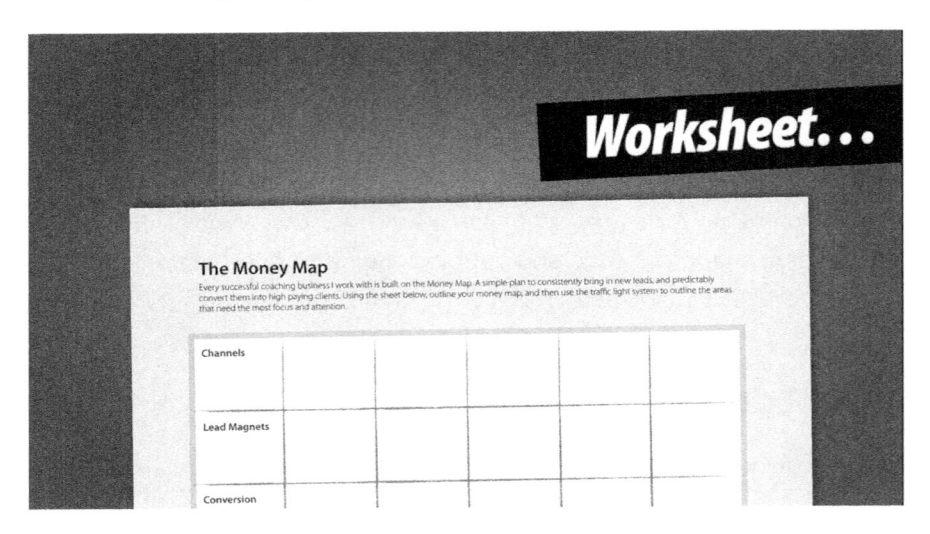

The Money Map is a simple plan to consistently bring in new leads and predictably convert them into high-paying clients. Every successful coaching business is built on a money map like this one. Here's how to use the Money Map to show how well your current funnel is generating money. First, list out all the channels you're currently using, your lead magnets, your conversions tools, your product(s), and your follow-up funnel.

Next, we introduce traffic lights: Shade anything that's working really well green. If it's not working at all, shade it red. If it's working a bit but could work better, shade it orange. The moment you complete your Money Map, you'll know what to work on first.

Our job is to create one green pathway from top to bottom. Start with the top row and find a green channel. If you've got a green channel, go down to the lead magnet row. If you haven't got anything green in the lead magnet, you'll have to tweak what you've got or build a new one. Your conversion tool can be a one-on-one meeting, a webinar, or an event. Hopefully, one of those is already working for you. If not, that's where you need to focus.

Build a clear green pathway from top to bottom, and you'll do really well.

Download the List-Building Essentials worksheet and the Money Map from www.MillionDollarCoach.com/kit.

Chapter 2: Build Authority

Notice the core word in "authority" is "author". Building authority is all about authoring the kind of content that establishes your expertise in your area. When it comes to your website, we want to author a specific kind of content — conversion content — that converts visitors into prospects.

There's so much confusion about websites. What goes on there and what doesn't? What should it look like? Who should I get to build it for me?

And because web development usually isn't our area, we're ignorant and vulnerable. I was on a Black Belt Q&A call (that's one of the webinars we run for our Black Belt clients) and someone had just been quoted $13,000 for a new website. $13,000!

My site brings in hundreds of thousands dollars in new leads every year and cost maybe $2,000 to build. A friend of mine, Dale, says web developers are like the 21st century's used car salespeople — it's hard to find one who's not trying to take you for a ride.

You know your website's important, but you don't know what to put on it, or how much it's supposed to cost.

I have a great client named Grant. When I first met him, he handed me a business card with his name on the front and nothing on the back. I said, "No contact details?" He goes, "Just Google me." The moment somebody hears about you, the first thing they do is jump on Google and type in your name. What they see next is critically important because it determines whether they go forward with you or not.

Now, most coaches I meet have good-looking — and sometimes very expensive — brochure sites, but their sites aren't generating leads at all. They're like ghost towns. It's really frustrating.

If you build your website right, and you fill it with the right kind of conversion content, it sets you up as the go-to guy or girl in your space, the one person I should come to for advice about how to solve the problems I need solving. It positions you as the guru sitting on top of a mountain. It positions you so well I'd climb buck naked over broken glass to meet you.

So your website's two main jobs are (1) positioning you as the absolute authority in your area and (2) collecting details from the people who'd like to meet you.

When your website works like this, people will come to depend on you. When I was a little kid at primary school, as soon as the school bell rang at the end of the day, my best friend David and I would high-five our friends, say goodbye to the teacher, chuck our backpacks on, and sprint the two blocks up the hill to my house. We'd run up the hill, around the corner, kick open this wooden gate where there'd be all these old figs that had fallen off the stupid fig tree that I hated. We'd reach under the wooden bench, find the little hook where dad hid the spare key, open up the door, run to the fridge to get some milk and some chocolate Milo, jump on the couch, and click on the remote control. If we timed it just right, the Batman theme music boomed out of the TV and we'd be like, "Yes, we made it!" and we'd watch the next exciting instalment of Batman. If we ever missed an episode, we'd be really bummed.

I do a podcast at salesmarketingprofit.com with my friend, James Shramko. Whenever I'm away or we don't record an episode, I come home to find messages for us asking, "When's the next episode coming out?" They're hungry for it. You want people in your world to be hungry for your next thing. www.salesmarketingprofit.com

Your website should be just like that, with people so hooked on your stuff they build their routine around it.

Todd

I want to introduce you to another one of my clients, Todd, in New York City. When I first met Todd, he was big in sports coaching and performance. He coached sports people and business people one on one, but he wanted to do something online.

I taught Todd how to unpack his ideas, his intellectual property — he had heaps, since he's a masterful guy — and helped him put together a series of videos with his business partner, Melanie, to position him as the expert in his field before he launched his program.

They showed the four videos over two weeks, and then announced his new program, The 90-Day Year. Some of the videos where shared by partners and included the partner. By the end of the launch, they'd signed up 225 clients at $2,000 each and done $450,000 in sales. (The program helps you get more done in 90 days than most people do in a year. It's epic, and you should check it out.) The next time Todd ran the program, he sold $550,000. Why? Because he'd become the obvious expert, the go-to guy in his market.

That happens when you build authority.

> What I want to do right now is find out from you: Why do you want to build authority in your space? I'm going to give you 20 seconds to write it down.
>
> Jamal says, *How do you build credibility if you're new to the coaching business?* Super easy, you don't talk about the results you've got because you haven't got any yet. Talk about the problems people have got instead. Wyatt Whitmore once said — and this is genius, "When you can articulate someone's problem better than they can, they automatically and unconsciously credit you with knowing the solution." So you don't need to talk about results. Just be the best at explaining their problem, and they will trust you to find the solution.

Engineer Next Actions

In Australia, we have these bush fire danger signs all through the country, anywhere there's a risk of a fire. The sign tells you what the fire danger is on any particular day, whether it's a low-risk or a high-risk day.

You can think about the people who visit your website, your prospects, a bit like this, too. They're way over on the left, cold and not ready to buy at all, or they're somewhere in the middle, or they're way over on the right, red hot.

Now, when it comes to making offers to website visitors, we usually make a big mistake: We assume everybody's ready to buy right now. We offer strategy sessions (code for "sales appointments") or send out "deal of the day" emails. These things are all about buying our stuff *right now*. That's fine for the 3% of visitors who are ready to make a decision, but what about everyone else?

We need different offers for the other 97%, so here's what you do. Make three offers on your website: a Green offer, a Yellow offer, and maybe a Red offer.

The Green offer is for people who are brand new, cold, and don't know you at all. They aren't ready for any kind of commitment. They want to check you out in a way that's safe for them. The Cheat Sheet we talked about earlier, your lead magnet, is the perfect Green offer for these guys.

The Yellow offer is for people who've been around you for a little while. They know who you are, and they're curious to learn more about your program and how it works. Your Yellow offer is your conversion tool: It's your webinar, your strategy session, or your event.

So the Green's job is to get an email address. The Yellow's job is to convert the email address into a prospect and sell them on the Red offer. The Red's job is to sell your product or coaching program.

If you visit my website at www.MillionDollarCoach.com, you'll see my Green offer (it's usually near the top on the right.) At the moment, it's The Triage Call PDF. There's a Yellow offer as well, which is an invitation to jump on my weekly webinar. In the webinar, I'll invite you to book in for an appointment.

So, think Green, Yellow, and Red when it comes to offers on your website, engineer a comfortable next action for each kind of visitor, and you'll be helping people take their first steps with you.

Maximise the Money Pages

Four pages on your website make a massive difference when it comes to converting visitors into leads. You've got to get these pages absolutely right, or frankly, you'll pay the price.

MAXIMISE THE 4 MONEY PAGES-OPT-IN, THANK YOU, VIDEO COURSE & WEBINAR.

The first page is the **opt-in page**. This is the page where they give you an email address in return for your lead magnet, your free thing. It's a dedicated page; it doesn't have all the navigation to the rest of your site, and its only job is to collect their email address. You need to obsess about the conversion rate of your opt-in page.

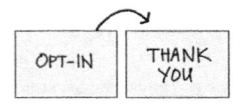

MAXIMISE THE 4 MONEY PAGES—OPT-IN, THANK YOU, VIDEO COURSE & WEBINAR.

The second page that matters a ton is the **thank you page**. Think about it for a moment: They've just given you their email address. What happens next is super important.

Now, 99 times out of a hundred, when I check someone's thank you page, it says something like, "Thanks so much for downloading my cool thing, please go check your email," or just as bad, "Thanks for requesting my cool thing, download it here." Let's just think about how mental this is. Of the billions of people in the world, and the millions of websites on the internet, I happen to land on yours and not only do I land on it, I'm one of the few percent of visitors who click on the link to your cool thing. It's the only time in the history of our relationship where you're 100% sure you've got my eyes on your stuff. You've got my complete and undivided attention, and I'm a bit excited about what comes next — and what do you do? You send me away. You send me away to my email inbox or my download folder, where everything else is clamouring for my attention, where all your competitors' stuff is too, and you've squandered a fantastic opportunity.

Here's what you do instead. What if you had a quick little video which says, "Hey, thanks so much for coming by and for requesting a copy of my Cool Thing™. It'll be in your inbox in about five minutes."

"While you're here though, I want to let you know about a special webinar I'm running for some of my clients later this week. We're going to cover X, Y, and Z and A, B, and C, and if you're interested in Cool Thing™, I think you'd love this too. If you'd like to join us, I'd love to give you a pass to come along as my guest. All you have to do is click the button below, get yourself registered, and I'll see you online really soon."

What did I just do? When I said, "Your Cool Thing™ will be in your inbox in five minutes," I bought myself five minutes of your time. You don't need to be anywhere for five minutes, so you might as well watch the video. And when I invite you to the webinar, I'm taking you from green to yellow in one easy move — there's no messy, drawn out follow-up.

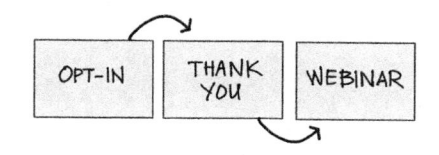

[OPT-IN] → [THANK YOU] → [WEBINAR]

MAXIMISE THE 4 MONEY PAGES—OPT-IN, THANK YOU, VIDEO COURSE & WEBINAR.

The opt-in page matters. The thank you page matters. Next, the webinar registration page matters too. And finally, there's a video course that helps us turn visitors into red-hot prospects.

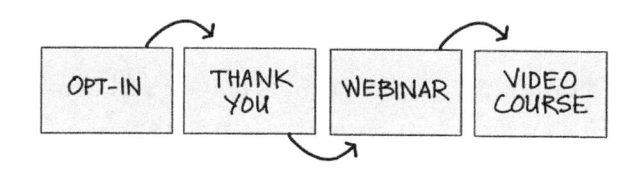

[OPT-IN] → [THANK YOU] → [WEBINAR] → [VIDEO COURSE]

MAXIMISE THE 4 MONEY PAGES—OPT-IN, THANK YOU, VIDEO COURSE & WEBINAR.

You might remember that in the previous chapter, I said video courses aren't great lead magnets. I did say that, but the order you do things in makes a difference: Offer the cheat sheet first, as it's the perfect first step. Then, on the thank you page, offer something a bit more intense, a bit more sales focused. Offer your coaching session, webinar, or live event and, hopefully, they'll take you up on that. If they don't, offer them the video course instead, and they'll become part of your ongoing follow-up.

Find Your Communication Rhythm

3 Find your Communication Rhythm

The whole idea behind building authority is offering useful content that gets people to do what you want them to do. It's conversion content, not just information.

Most coaches' communication rhythm is patchy and inconsistent, and they don't follow up anywhere near as much as they should. For your audience, that's a bit like listening to a musician who's off-key and can't keep time. I want to show you how to find your communication rhythm instead. If you follow these four follow-up commitments, and you find a rhythm you can commit to, you'll do incredibly well.

(FREQUENCY)

FIND YOUR COMMUNICATION RHYTHM—4 FOLLOW-UP COMMITMENTS.

The first commitment I want you to make is the commitment to **frequency**. Commit to publishing useful content regularly.

How frequently should you publish? Well, for starters, once every three months isn't nearly enough. (Not even close. That quarterly newsletter you were thinking about? Forget it.) Even if you send something out once a month, only 20-30% of people will open your emails, so they're effectively only hearing from you every three to five months, which still isn't enough.

You want to be sending fresh, engaging content *at least* once every two weeks. Ideally, it's once a week. (For some of you, it could be a few times a week, or even daily.) How do you choose? Choose the highest frequency you can deliver consistently.

Committing to frequency isn't just about how often you publish; it's about the medium you choose, too. Choose video, audio, or written form, whichever one is easiest for you, and stick to it.

I do podcasts because they're really just conversations, which are easy for me. I love doing my weekly videos as well, either quick and easy with a phone and a selfie-stick, or more full-on with a Canon camera and a tripod. I don't do any written content anymore because I find writing hard. But if writing works best for you, or you don't love being in front of a camera, then write!

> I just want to know, do you feel most comfortable doing video or audio, or writing? Take a moment right now and write your preference down. What's it going to be? Video, audio, or text?

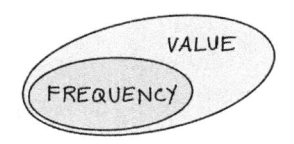

FIND YOUR COMMUNICATION RHYTHYM-4 FOLLOW-UP COMMITMENTS.

Next, commit to **value**. If you're sending your stuff out regularly, but all you're sending is "Hey, buy my stuff. Hey, it's me again, buy my stuff. Hey, still me, buy my stuff," you'll lose people very quickly. Send me two of those emails, and I'm done. Unsubscribe!

How do you make your stuff really, really valuable? Simple. Keep track of the biggest issues your current clients are struggling with right now, today, and use those topics in your marketing. Every two weeks, I run a webinar with my clients, chatting about the issues they're facing and helping them solve their problems. I'm answering their questions and writing down the answers, and guess what? All these things become weekly videos on my blog.

My friend, James Schramko, coined a term for this: "news trap". News traps help you collect the topics you can write or talk about in your videos, audios, and articles. The easiest way to guarantee your content is valuable is by solving real problems for real people, so think about how (or where) you can set your own news traps. Let your current clients help you find new ones.

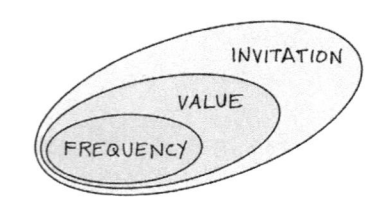

FIND YOUR COMMUNICATION RHYTHYM-4 FOLLOW-UP COMMITMENTS.

Thirdly, commit to sending **invitations**. Every email, every piece of content you post on your blog (whether it's written or recorded) should have a clear invitation to take the next step with you. I challenge you to find one video on my www.MillionDollarCoach.com blog that doesn't mention a service or a next step that you could take with me.

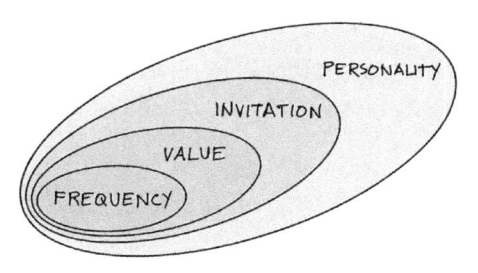

FIND YOUR COMMUNICATION RHYTHM-4 FOLLOW-UP COMMITMENTS.

Fourthly, commit to **personality**. Take your authenticity and amplify it. If you talk quickly and have loads of energy, be like that. If you're quiet, formal and corporate, then be like that. If you're an accountant and you love your pocket protector, then wear it with pride. Commit to being yourself at your very best.

> I've got a question for you right now. What are three words that describe you when you're at your best? Just take 30 seconds right now and write them down. Three words to describe you at your best.
>
> Out of those three key principles — engineering next actions, maximizing those four money pages, or finding your communication rhythm — which one do you need most right now? Just take a moment and write down which one of these three is going to be most useful for you.
>
> *Communication rhythm. My thank you page sucks right now. Engineer the next actions. Solve real people's real problems.*
>
> Okay, Tim's asking, *What news traps do I use?* Mate, webinars and fortnightly Q&A calls are more than enough. I create a video and a podcast regularly; they're the main things I do. All the other content I create comes straight out of Black Belt.

When a client has a win, then I do a case study about them, that's a podcast or a client interview. I only need one news trap, and that's the work I'm doing with my clients because I've got kick-ass clients, who kick ass regularly!

Green, yellow and red offers. Optimising the thank you page was great, thank you!

What do you need from me right now in terms of building authority? I'm really able to talk about video because it's one of my favourites. I can talk about technology too, if you want. What do you need to know in order to get really good at this authority building piece?

A clear structure to get started. Developing communications from client situations has been really helpful.

Here's my blog. Let just talk about what's going on here. The moment you land on a website, the first thing you ask is, "Does this page look like it's here to take something from me or give something to me?" Because the content is front and centre, and it's all problem-solving content, it looks like it's here to give me something. There's no obvious opt-in form anywhere, just cool stuff that I can do. So that's the content. Here's the lead magnet, The Triage Call guide, where people can opt in. That's my green offer.

There's a webinar, the free training webinar, Million Dollar Coach, which is my yellow offer. There's an event in Sydney and Santa Monica, or one of our other US locations. You'll see case studies, stories, all collected through my news traps. Here's how to make every video a call-to-action machine, let's just click on a video, see what happens.

It's got video on top, audio underneath, text below (just transcribed). Let's see what happens when we click play. All right, let's just pause, ten seconds in, a call to action pops up for my yellow offer, "A free online webinar about how to market and sell with webinars. Click here for the details." The best place to check this stuff out is www.MillionDollarCoach.com.

Sandy, does that help?

Ideas for the thank you page? Mate, I can show you exactly how to smash a thank you page. Here's my best, highest-converting thank you page for The Triage Call. I don't know if this one is going to let me load it right now, it's got a timer attached to it. Mate, if you opt in for The Triage Call guide, that's the bit; just click through, you'll see the thank you page right there.

Can you explain news traps again? Yeah man, you want to have a list of places where your clients can basically spoon-feed you content for your marketing. Any time you're talking with them, you can be potentially collecting great content.

How to Build Your Green, Yellow, and Red Offers

First, decide what your green, yellow, and red offers will be. Choose your three offers. The green opt-in bribe, the yellow conversion tool, and the red product or program you want people to buy. (Hint: It's not okay to say you've got ten programs to choose from. Pick one!)

Next, decide your communication frequency — weekly ideally, fortnightly at least — and the media you'll work in. Obviously, if you choose video, there's a structure for creating a video with the right kind of flow. If you choose audio, there's a framework for delivering a great piece of audio content. If you choose to write articles, there are seven content funnels we use for writing stories. Commit to frequency, find the framework that fits, then set your news traps. Decide when and where you're going to collect ideas for your content so you're never short of things to talk or write about.

I've created a couple of worksheets you can download to help with all of this: Two Offers You Must Make on Your Authority Site, and Frequency and Media Foundational Decisions.

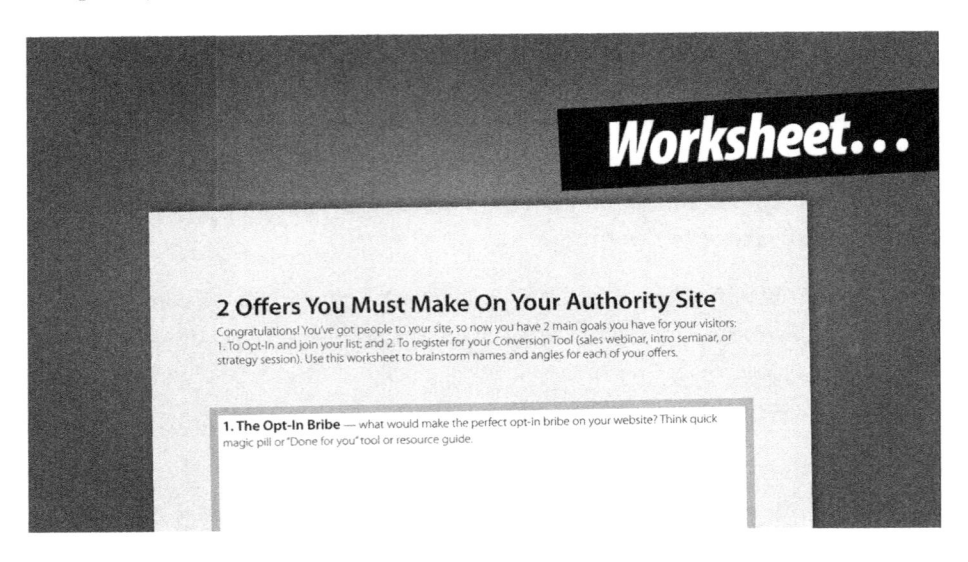

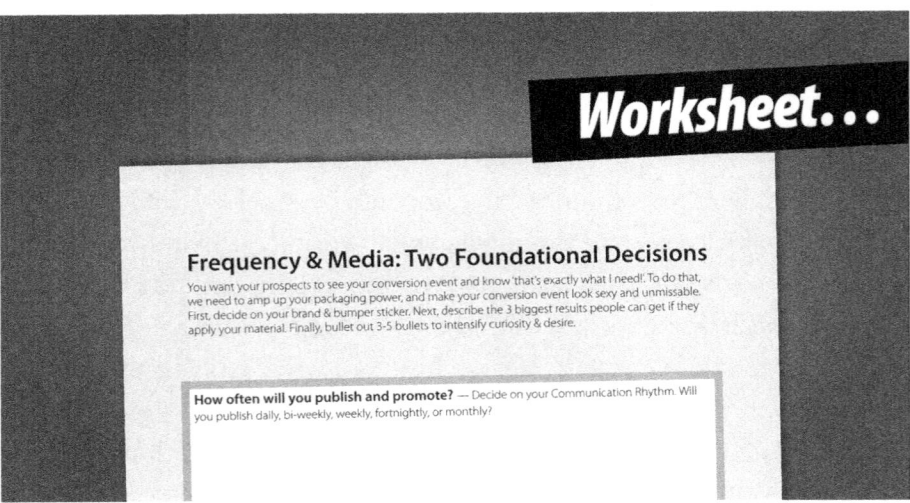

Worksheet...

2 Offers You Must Make On Your Authority Site

Congratulations! You've got people to your site, so now you have 2 main goals you have for your visitors: 1. To Opt-In and join your list; and 2. To register for your Conversion Tool (sales webinar, intro seminar, or strategy session). Use this worksheet to brainstorm names and angles for each of your offers.

1. The Opt-In Bribe — what would make the perfect opt-in bribe on your website? Think quick magic pill or "Done for you" tool or resource guide.

Worksheet...

Frequency & Media: Two Foundational Decisions

You want your prospects to see your conversion event and know 'that's exactly what I need!'. To do that, we need to amp up your packaging power, and make your conversion event look sexy and unmissable. First, decide on your brand & bumper sticker. Next, describe the 3 biggest results people can get if they apply your material. Finally, bullet out 3-5 bullets to intensify curiosity & desire.

How often will you publish and promote? — Decide on your Communication Rhythm. Will you publish daily, bi-weekly, weekly, fortnightly, or monthly?

Chapter 3: Install Automation

When you think about all the great civilisations in history, they weren't hunters; they were builders. The Egyptians, the Romans, the Greeks; they all built. They built aqueducts, they built roads, and they built systems that brought the results they needed right to their front door.

You don't want to be a hunter. Sure, it's fun sometimes, hunting in the jungle, bringing back a wildebeest. But sooner or later, you'll get sick of having to go out there every day, especially when you're coming home empty-handed.

Imagine you're living in a village, walking miles every day just to fetch water. If you're entrepreneurial, you could build a good little business with a couple of buckets, ferrying water from the creek. When you got back to the village, you'd sell your water instantly because it's such a pain to fetch yourself and everybody needs water. You could start your business with very few resources, start making money right away. But here's the thing: Eventually, you're going to get tired. There's only so many trips you can do in a day before you burn out.

And the moment someone comes along with a pipeline, you're out of business. First, you're exhausted long before they are. You can try harder and harder, but the pipeline will always provide faster, cheaper, and higher-quality water than you and your buckets.

That's what it's like in a coaching business. At its most basic level, a coaching business is a coach and a client, and the coach is running solutions back and forth like buckets from the well. It's fun at first; it's fast. It's all good until you run out of energy, until you get tired.

Instead of running back and forth, it's much better to build a pipeline in your business. One that brings leads, prospects, sales appointments, and ultimately dollars into your business more quickly and cheaply, and of better quality than you could do on your own.

We're going to build that pipeline.

Raj

I've got a great client in San Francisco, called Raj. He works with lawyers, and he's a complete legend. When he was a lawyer (in his previous life), he realised what it was like to have a business that depended entirely on him. When he got out of lawyering, he decided to build a business that didn't depend on him at all.

Today, Raj has leveraged his lead generation with authority marketing and paid traffic. New people flow into his world regularly. They love his authority content, and they jump on his webinar. At the end of the webinar, they book in for a Triage Call or a Strategy Session with his sales team. They sign up for his group coaching program, which has three years of curriculum completely built out and systemised, with a totally automated delivery system. He's not needed at all. Raj's only commitment is 90 minutes every three or four weeks, when he shows up for the program's Q&A phone hook-up.

The whole machine gives him more of what he wants and less of what he doesn't, and it gives his clients an incredible outcome. It's seamless all the way through, from attract through convert to deliver, and it's beautiful.

> What I want to know right now is this: If you could generate leads and new clients every single week, what would that give you? Why do you want to automate your marketing? I'm going to give you 60 seconds right now to write down your answers.

You need three things to install automation in your business: a system that works, a way to automate everything so it works consistently, and a way to improve the system so it works better for you the more you use it.

Work Hard Once

I can hear you thinking, *Isn't it lots of hard work pulling all of this together?* Absolutely, yes, it's loads of work. But here's the thing: You're already working hard. There's a difference between my hard work and your hard work: You have to work hard every damn day, or everything grinds to a halt. I work hard once to build a system that stays built and works for me forever, even when I'm on holidays or enjoying time off with my family.

There is a Chinese proverb that says, "The best time to plant an oak tree is 20 years ago." If you planted your tree all the way back then, you could be sitting under your tree right now enjoying its shade. "The second best time to plant an oak tree is today." The best time to automate your marketing was when you first started marketing — imagine what it could have been like today! But if you didn't do it then, the next best time to automate your marketing is right now.

You might work some late nights or weekends. It's worth it. When you're kicking back on a tropical island with an ice-cold, fruity drink in your hand, and the leads are still rolling in to your business, those late nights will seem totally worth it.

Be the Architect

There's lots of work to do, but you don't have to do it all yourself. You don't even have to know how to build it all yourself. Your job is to know what you want, why you want it, and how to get the right bodies to build it for you. And that's way less expensive than you think. (I'll show you how in the Leverage Talent chapter in the next section.)

Your job is to be the thinker, the designer, the architect. I do most of my work sitting in cafes, scribbling in notebooks with big, fat markers. Why? Because I'm the architect. My job is to sketch out the designs, then communicate them with the team who bring those plans to life.

Don't be the guy or gal who tries to build everything themselves. Real value lies in finding the right heads and the right hands. Find the right people who can guide you (the heads) and the right people who can build this stuff for you at a reasonable price (the hands). I'm happy to pay a premium for the heads to get the very best advice, and I try to be smart about the hands, to get the building done as economically as possible. That's exactly how I built my business.

Pave Their Path

When you're building an automated marketing system, your job is to always be thinking a few steps ahead of your prospects. You want to pave their path. When my son, Jotham, was young, maybe seven or so, we were on holidays up in Queensland, and there were these two old guys playing chess.

I don't know if you've ever watched old guys playing chess, but it's a slow game. Jotham has full-on ADD, so he was watching them, then getting distracted, then watching, then getting distracted again. These old guys were taking ages to make a move, but Jotham was fascinated by the strategy of the game.

Eventually, one of the old guys asked Jotham if he wanted to play. Jotham went first, just pushed a piece out onto the board. The old guy took forever to reply. While he was thinking, Jotham looked in the other direction, totally distracted. Eventually, the old guy made his move and Jotham immediately picked up a piece, moved it forward, and went back to looking the other way.

This went on for a while, and eventually my wife said, "Jotham, how are you doing this? You're not even paying attention." Jotham said, point blank, "I don't need to look at the game. I already know what he's going to do, and what I'm going to do, and what he'll do next." Jotham was automatically thinking two or three moves ahead.

That's how you want to be when you map out your marketing system, like a chess master. For each step in your system, you want to think through the next step and the one after that. What do you want them to think? How do you want them to feel? What do you want them to do?

I heard that Alfred Hitchcock created two scripts for his movies, a brown script and a blue script. The brown script was a standard movie script — WOMAN taking shower silhouetted behind a shower curtain, PSYCHO creeps up wielding huge, scary knife — that sort of thing.

The blue script described how Hitchcock wanted his audience to feel at that particular place in the movie. The blue script set the tone, the mood.

When you define marketing sequences, you want to describe where your prospects are and what's happening at any given point in the process. You also want to describe what you want them to think, how you want them to feel, and specifically what you want them to do next. The trick is to think ahead, to think through the next moves like a chess master.

The Marketing Automation Checklist

When it comes to building automated systems, here's a really helpful checklist of 15 or 16 mini-campaigns we run with our Black Belt clients. The first step is to look down the list and tick anything you're already running as an automated system. Then look through the rest of the list and choose the top five strategies most likely to have the biggest impact in your business right now. Those are your marketing automation projects for the next 90 days. Install those first five and start building yourself some freedom.

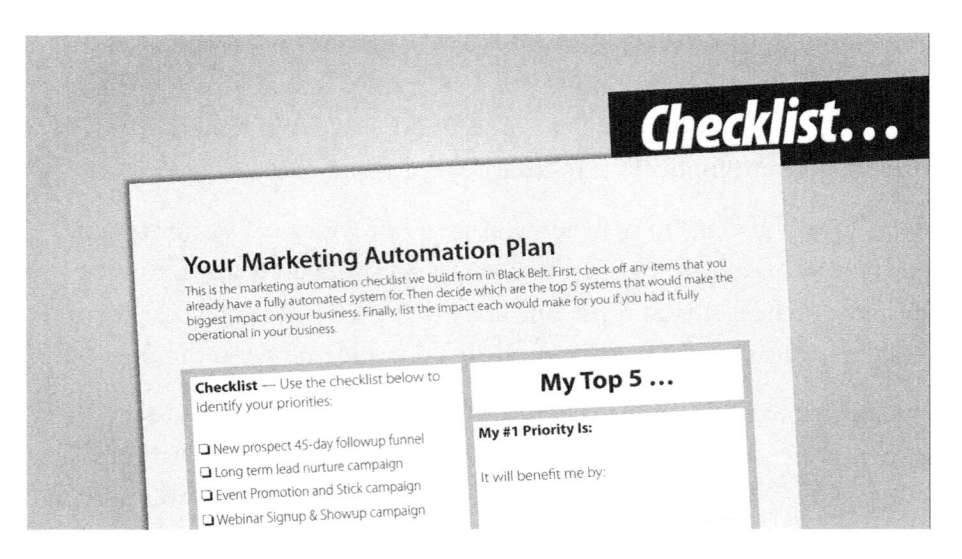

Checklist...

Your Marketing Automation Plan

This is the marketing automation checklist we build from in Black Belt. First, check off any items that you already have a fully automated system for. Then decide which are the top 5 systems that would make the biggest impact on your business. Finally, list the impact each would make for you if you had it fully operational in your business.

Checklist — Use the checklist below to identify your priorities:

- ❏ New prospect 45-day followup funnel
- ❏ Long term lead nurture campaign
- ❏ Event Promotion and Stick campaign
- ❏ Webinar Signup & Showup campaign

My Top 5 ...

My #1 Priority Is:

It will benefit me by:

You can download The Marketing Automation Plan from www.MillionDollarCoach.com/kit.

What software do you use for your automations, for managing your systems? I use Ontraport. You can use InfusionSoft or ActiveCampaign. I use WordPress for my website, and the MemberMouse plug-in for managing our membership.

PART TWO

CONVERT

Chapter 4: Audition Clients

Here's the problem: When you're selling your stuff one-on-one, you get to the point where you're about to ask for the sale, and there's a whole bunch of pressure. There's pressure on you to perform, to close the deal and sign the client. Maybe there's pressure on you from home to come back with the money today. There's pressure on the prospect, too. They're sitting there, feeling like they're just a sales opportunity for you, so even before they start the meeting, they've got their back up a little bit. They're defensive. There's pressure on you; there's pressure on them; there's pressure on the whole conversation. Pressure is no way to start any kind of working relationship.

My 'sherpa,' Adam, works with me on my Black Belt program. He's an amazing coach and a great guy. He was in a sales appointment recently where the prospect was being really defensive, giving one-word answers, and it just felt weird and wrong. Instead of ignoring the awkwardness and pushing ahead, Adam did what anyone should do in this situation. He said, "I don't know how this feels for you, but it feels all wrong for me. This feels like you think you're in a sales conversation and you've got your defences up, and I just want to let you know up front that's not how we roll here. I want to have a simple conversation with you and work out if we're a match or not. If we're a match, we'll do something together. If we're not, of course we won't; there's no pressure, there's no need for any of this weirdness. If that's not how you'd like this conversation to go, then why don't we stop right now and walk away as friends."

Pulling the escape hatch like this released all the pressure from the conversation. The guy relaxed and started to lean in, and they ended up having an amazing conversation. The guy became a great client.

To let that happen, we had to remove the pressure.

Here's something else that goes wrong in one-on-one selling situations: objections, excuses, and stalls. You get pushback. Just think about that expression for a second: *pushback*. If you ever feel your prospect pushing back, understand that at some level they feel like you pushed them first. If you get any pushback, it's a great sign that you're doing something wrong.

And finally, the big risk at the end of your conversation is that, instead of walking away with a great new client, you get a no. All of a sudden you're in this really weird position. You can do what you've been taught to do, push hard and use all the manipulative techniques you know to close the deal. Or you can be the nice guy, take the no at face value and walk away from the sale. You're in a weird place where you have to decide: Am I going to be a douchebag, a pushy sales person? Or am I going to be a loser and walk away with nothing?

Well, hopefully, there's a third option, right?

When you avoid the traditional one-on-one approach to selling, it's a really different story. Instead of pressure and awkwardness, you can have a natural, calm, easy conversation. "Our job today is to work out if we're a match or not." Just be really calm, no need to push. No need for high energy, or anything like that. Imagine a balloon that's been blown up to bursting, then had all its air let out. There's no pent-up energy; there's no force in it. When you take away the pressure, it's just a simple, casual chat.

Instead of working hard to impress your prospect, you become the judge. You're not singing your heart out on the American Idol stage, you're Simon Cowell on the judging panel assessing your prospect's audition. You're the one who decides if your prospect's coming to Hollywood or if they're going home. You're the one assessing the auditions, so you're in the power position, not the begging position.

When you do this process well, your prospects buy from you. You don't have to sell to them. There are no closing questions anywhere in this whole conversation, there's just a purchase at the end. It's all about them buying, not about you selling. If you can do this right, you'll find that you'll easily sign 80% of your prospects (or more) into your coaching program, without any kind of threat, without any pushing, without any manipulation at all.

What would a sales process like this do for you? If you could have a really casual, relaxed chat with someone about whether they are a fit or not, and have 80% of the people say, "Can I work with you? I am ready, credit card in hand," at the end. What would that do for you?

That would give me ease, would change my life, way less pressure. Sounds dreamy. Ryan, you are dreamy. Cindy says, *Comfort. Easy peasy*, says Louise. Great to have you here, mate. *Why start making it simple? Lots of fun. It would be life changing,* totally. *It would align with my value system.* Yeah, you can be yourself. Trevor says, *I've been using it since learning it from you and it works.* Totally, it works. *Way more confidence, more fun.* Great to hear that, man. *It would be a relief to remove the pressure. Boost my business.* Right, it takes the stress right out.

Tristan

I want to introduce you to one of my clients, a great guy. His name is Tristan. When I met him, about a year and a half ago now, his business had plateaued, and he was frustrated. He was trying to do all the right things, but he was running webinars and having sales conversations without any proper structure. He was winging it.

Tristan's income was stuck around the $13-$15,000 a month mark. If he marketed, his client numbers went up, his income went up, his confidence went sky high, ... and then he'd lose it. He'd take his foot off the marketing accelerator, lose a client or two, and his income dropped back down again. Then he'd fire up the marketing, and he was back on the roller coaster, hitting up against this $15,000 threshold. It was frustrating and annoying.

I showed him two things. First, I showed him how to do a webinar that rocks (I'll show you too in two chapters' time.) Second, I taught him how to do strategy sessions really, really well.

More than anybody, Tristan embodies the **don't impress, but assess** principle. He's practically channelling Simon Cowell; he's a complete boss. In fact, if I open up my phone right now, I can show you text message after text message:

"Bam, the closing machine strikes again."

"Bam, new client."

"Bam!"

Here's the thing. Tristan's first webinar was a joint venture with a partner who specifically said, "No sales!" He wasn't allowed to sell anything at all. So we put together a really nice offer for some free content. The offer included an eBook, an audio recording, and a diagnostic audit, which was basically just a conversation with Tristan, a strategy session.

Instead of winging it, Tristan used the webinar to set up his offer, which he used to set up the strategy sessions, which he then nailed.

That first webinar, he made $336,000 in sales. Imagine you had a client who was stuck at $15,000 a month and then, 30 days later, runs his first webinar (where he's not even allowed to sell anything!), and he makes over three hundred thousand dollars and pays off his mortgage. What a boss.

The Perfect Prospect Pipeline

We use a four-step framework called **The Perfect Prospect Pipeline** to audition clients:

```
INDOCTRINATION
     EVENT
```

THE PERFECT PIPELINE-A FRAMEWORK FOR AUDITIONING CLIENTS.

The first step is an **indoctrination event** — a webinar, a live event, or a series of videos aimed at pre-selling your stuff, getting people hungry, thirsty, and wanting what you got. At the end of your indoctrination event, you're going to invite people to take a next step with you. Heaps of people will want it, but not everybody will be a qualified fit.

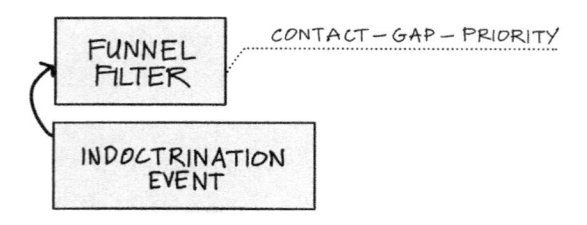

```
  FUNNEL          CONTACT - GAP - PRIORITY
  FILTER
INDOCTRINATION
     EVENT
```

THE PERFECT PIPELINE-A FRAMEWORK FOR AUDITIONING CLIENTS.

The second step is a **funnel filter**. The funnel filter's job is to qualify people in or out so you can quickly work out who's a match and who isn't. It's a simple online form they fill in, where they can click a button to book into your calendar.

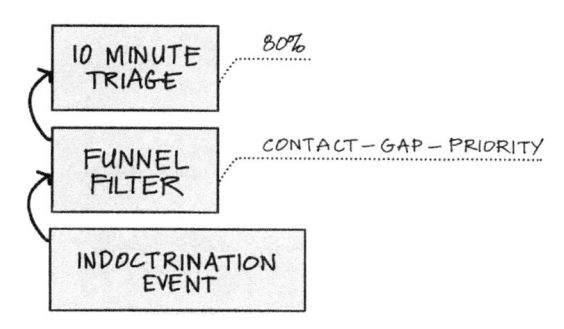

```
    10 MINUTE        80%
     TRIAGE

     FUNNEL          CONTACT - GAP - PRIORITY
     FILTER

   INDOCTRINATION
       EVENT
```

THE PERFECT PIPELINE - A FRAMEWORK FOR AUDITIONING CLIENTS.

The third step is a 10-minute **Triage Call**, which is our name for an audition. It's a 10-minute phone conversation that has two jobs: Number one, it builds trust as fast as possible. Number two, it qualifies people in or out. The Triage Call clearly positions you as the expert in your field, and at the end of the call, you decide whether or not they move on to the next step.

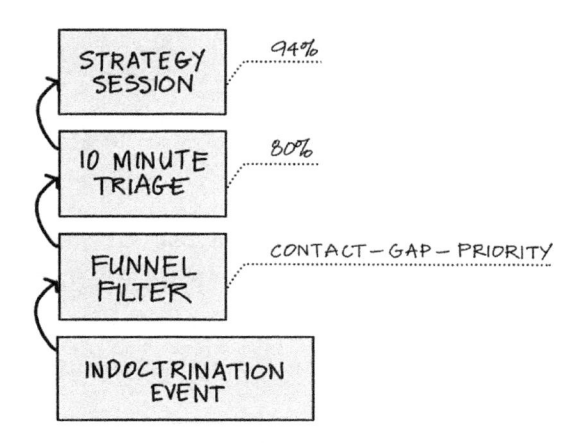

```
    STRATEGY         94%
    SESSION

    10 MINUTE        80%
     TRIAGE

     FUNNEL          CONTACT - GAP - PRIORITY
     FILTER

   INDOCTRINATION
       EVENT
```

THE PERFECT PIPELINE - A FRAMEWORK FOR AUDITIONING CLIENTS.

The last step is **The Strategy Session**. It's a 45-minute conversation with you, or someone on your sales team. About 80% of the people you talk to in the Strategy Session pass their audition because the indoctrination event, the funnel filter, and the triage call all have done their job. In our world, 94% of the people we talk to at Black Belt strategy sessions become clients. Your numbers will vary, of course (especially when you're brand new), but 80-94% gives you a fair idea of what you can expect.

If you want to run killer Strategy Sessions like Tristan, there are three things you need to know.

Lead the Prospect

When your prospect shows up for a strategy session, they have no idea how it's supposed to go. They're a little bit nervous, they're a little bit defensive, and frankly, they'd prefer if they could just get some free information from you without having to buy anything.

We need to take care of those three things in the first three minutes. Our goal is to make people feel comfortable (not defensive), to have them trust the process (and open up), and to get them telling you why they need your help right now (in other words, why they need more than just some free information).

The first thing we do is build rapport. Take 30 seconds, 60 seconds at the most, and make some small talk just to get the conversation started. The second thing we do is lay out the agenda. And the third thing we do is ask *the decision question* — the question that gets people talking about why they need you right now.

At the end of these three minutes, you're in a really good place because they're comfortable and will have opened up. They know how it's going to go; they know they can trust the process. They feel like they can lower their defences a bit, be open, and lean into the process. They get heaps out of it this way, whether they buy from you or not.

The decision question reveals the number one issue that needs fixing *right now*. I call it the $100,000 problem. Coaches and consultants always freak out about the cost of their programs. What if it's too expensive? What if people say 'no' because the price is too high?

I want you to stop thinking for a second about the cost of your program, and start thinking about the cost of not doing your program. If I've got a $100,000 problem and you've got a $10,000 solution; you're a walking, talking good deal, and I'd buy it in a heartbeat.

Stretch the Gap

Stretching the gap is the longest part of our 45-minute conversation, which usually takes about half an hour, maybe a bit longer. There are three parts to stretching the gap. Think of it as a big rubber band: There's the left end, the right end, and the rubber in the middle.

People hire a coach when there's tension, when there's a gap between where they are now and where they want to be. They're stuck because there are roadblocks in the way. Understanding these three parts of their story gets you hired every single time.

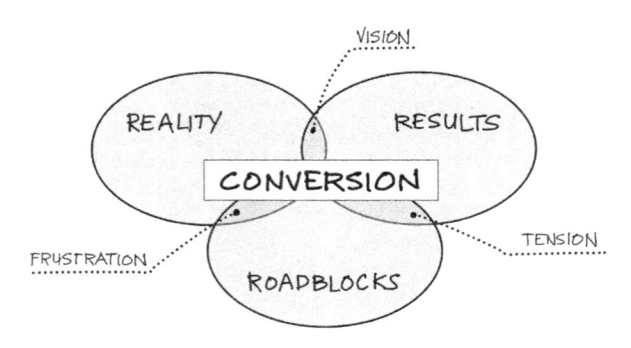

STRETCH THE GAP—UNDERSTAND THE 3 KEY PARTS OF THEIR STORY.

In the conversion conversation, our job is to stretch the gap. We don't have to dig for pain or twist any knives. Our job is to identify a gap that already exists, that's real for them right now. We want them to acknowledge it, become fully present to it, and really feel it.

Imagine you have a big fat rubber band (like the one in the picture). The first thing that we're going to do is look at their desired result, where they want to go. It's like you're stretching the rubber band out to the right. We're creating a little bit of tension in this rubber band now — not a heap, but some — by getting clear about where they want to go.

Then we're going to look at where they are at right now. It's like pulling the rubber band back to the left. Ask them a question like, "So what's it like for you right now?" They'll tell you where they are, and boom, there's real tension in this rubber band. You know where they want to go, and you know where they are right now.

Next, we're going to make a list of all the things that are holding them back. Every answer they give us stretches that gap out heaps until there's all this tension in there that needs to be relieved.

The best, fastest, and only way they can relieve that tension is by talking to the person who's helping them hold the ends of this big rubber band, the person who understands exactly where they are, where they want to go, and all the things that are holding them back.

That person is you.

When you help them get really clear about those three things, you create an incredible sense of vision and possibility. You create excitement. When you're really clear about the results they want and the things that are holding them back, you create the kind of tension that drives people to take action.

Get Hired

The third key is getting hired. Let me be really clear about an important difference here. The first two keys are things that you do. You lead the prospect. You stretch the gap. You're instigating those things. But hiring you isn't something you do, it's something they do — and it's the fun part of this whole convert piece.

Instead of 30 minutes of finding out about them, then saying "Great, now it's my turn to talk," and blabbing on about your stuff, telling them everything (you think) they need to know about you and your program, as well as a bunch of stuff they never wanted to hear, you're going to have a really simple conversation.

At the end of this conversation, they're going to ask, "Can you help me with this?" or "How does it work?" or "What do you think I should do?" And the way you tell them is by giving them these six magic pills, one pill at a time.

Each of these magic pills only goes for about a minute, so they're quick and easy to dispense. We're going to give them a pill, then we're going to check in with them by asking a very specific, three-question loop. This loop gets them feeling present and safe, and it gets them wanting you to give them the next pill. You're not pushing anything down their throat; they're leaning in, asking for your help. That's how you get hired.

There are three questions we need to answer in this piece:

- Why should I hire you?
- What are we going to work on together?
- How does your program work?

How to respond to those why, what, and how questions is what we're going to talk about now.

SIX MAGIC PILLS—HOW TO GET HIRED.

The first pill is the **problem**. When they get to the part where they say, "How can you help me?", we're going to go deep on their three biggest problems and the impact those problems are having on their business or life. You'll say something like, "From what you've said so far, it sounds like the biggest problem you're having is … and that's causing you to …." When you say it this way, they will feel like you really get them.

Then we do our three-question loop. Ask them: "Is this making sense?" (Wait for them to answer.) "Are you 100% comfortable with everything so far?" (Wait for them to answer.) "Where do you think we should go from here?" (And wait for them to answer.)

The three-question loop helps them feel like they're in control, even though you're the one directing the conversation.

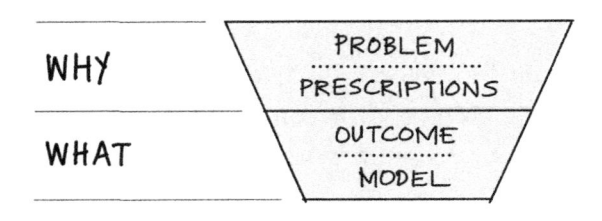

```
                        PROBLEM
   WHY            .....................
                       PRESCRIPTIONS
   ─────────          ─────────────
                        OUTCOME
   WHAT           .....................
                         MODEL
```

SIX MAGIC PILLS—HOW TO GET HIRED.

The second pill is **prescriptions**. Here's where we tell them what they need. You say something like, "You need a ... that will help you with ..." And you repeat the thing that they need to help them solve each of the problems you mentioned in step one. Then you do your three-question loop again. You give them the what, but not the how.

Those few things get people hooked on the *why*.

Next, tell them the outcomes they can expect from joining your program. Most people jump straight into logistics, the details about how their program works: "We have a session every week, and we meet together here, and ..." It's boring. Logistics are the least sexy, least exciting part of your program. Don't talk about logistics; talk about outcomes.

For example, we run a nine-week program called Million Dollar Coach Implementation Program, in which we show you everything you need to know to get your business to $10,000 a month. The outcome is really simple: "Become a $10,000-a-month coach."

In our Black Belt program, the outcome is "Double your income, double your time off. Get to $1,000,000 a year and beyond." Those outcomes are really clear. People buy outcomes, not logistics, so explain your outcomes first. Then you ask your three-question loop again.

Next they're going to ask, "How does it work?" **Teach them your model**. Draw a diagram, a simple graphical representation, explaining how your thing works, piece by piece. Make sure your diagram is a simple arrangement of circles, triangles, or squares — simple enough so you could explain how to draw it over the phone. It shows people the three to five, maybe six, core things you'd work on together.

After you've taught them your model, ask your three-question loop again. That takes care of the *what*.

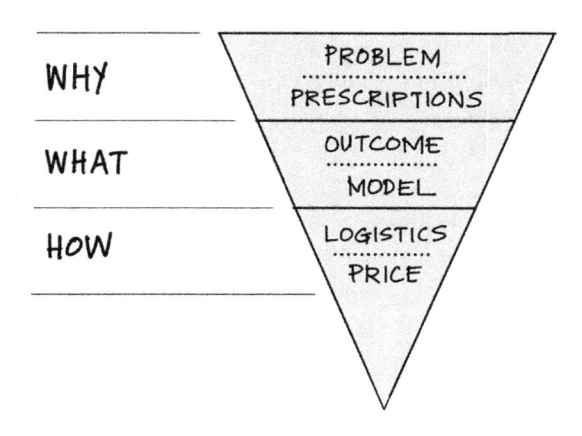

```
WHY     | PROBLEM
        | PRESCRIPTIONS
WHAT    | OUTCOME
        | MODEL
HOW     | LOGISTICS
        | PRICE
```

SIX MAGIC PILLS–HOW TO GET HIRED.

Now you can talk about **logistics** — but let's package them up in a specific way so you don't just blab on about deliverables and bore people to death. Organise your stuff into three buckets: Our buckets are *The Plan* (how they get clear about what to do next and get up to speed), *The System* (how you deliver your training), and *The Help* (where they go, who they talk to, and how they get help when they need it). Use whatever buckets make sense for your program; just make sure you organise them around your customer's needs.

Then ask your three-question loop again.

Finally, we get to the price. Tell them how much it is. Once you've told them the price, ask them the third question in the three-question loop, "Where do you think we should go from here?" Eighty percent (or more) of people are going to say, "Well, that all sounds great, how do I get started?" And away you go.

> Super quick recap. There are three keys to auditioning clients. Number one, lead the prospect. Make them feel safe. Give them the agenda. Ask the decision question. Number two, stretch the gap. Get clear about their results, where they want to go. Uncover their current reality. Identify the roadblocks. Number three, get yourself hired. What I want to know right now is, which one of those three was most valuable for you? Which one of those three did you need most in your world right now?
>
> *Education-based marketing. Doesn't the three-question loop get redundant?* Nope. Here's the thing: The whole conversation is about them. Every single word you say is about them and what their situation is, respectfully. Here's what I think is redundant: manipulating people into doing stuff they don't want to do. Mr. Prospect, would you like that in red or black? Or any one of those manipulative false choice closes where we push people down directions they don't want to go in. Just because they are weak and defenceless, we push them into stuff that isn't right for them.

How to Run Your Strategy Session

Let's talk about the mechanics and specific details of the strategy session. I said earlier there are three keys to a strategy session: Lead The Prospect, Stretch The Gap, and Get Hired. Each one of those keys has three moves, so there are nine steps in any strategy session. The good news is, there's no script to memorise; just keep this model in mind.

HOW TO RUN A STRATEGY SESSION—9 STEPS TO GETTING HIRED.

The first step is building rapport. It's so basic, I'm sure you've done heaps of training on rapport, or you're just naturally good with people. Actually, that's the problem right there. The trick with rapport is keeping it short, 30 seconds, a minute tops. I think, "Ask them about their cat." (It doesn't have to be their cat, obviously.) Just ask them something relevant to get the conversation started, then move on to the next step.

The second thing we want to do is lay out the agenda. I say, "There's a framework I like to use for conversations like this, just to make sure we both walk out of here with a really clear plan. There are three things that I want to do today. Number one, I'd love to get super clear about where you want to go and what results you're after. The clearer I am about where you want to go, the easier it's going to be for me to help you get a plan together. Is that cool?" They say, "Sure."

"The second thing I'd love to do, is talk about how it is right now, your current reality. I want to know the lay of the land, what's working, what's not working, everything you've tried so far. Once I am clear about what's really going on, then I'll know what we've got to work with and what it's going to take to get you to the goals. Okay?"

"Thirdly, once I know where you are and where you want to go, then let's identify all the roadblocks, all the things that are stopping you, so we can turn that into our action plan. Are you cool with that?" They'll say, "Sure."

Then I say, "This conversation is about you, it's not about me. If you want to go over here or over there, or talk about something else you think is important, that's completely cool; you take this wherever you want it to go. I want you to walk out of here really clear about what to do next. Is that fine?" They'll say, "Sure."

What have I just done? I've given them an overview of how it's going to go; they know what's going to happen so they don't have to resist, and they can just trust the process. Next, I've given them complete control (or at least a sense of control). The moment they feel like they have enough control to take the conversation where they want, they don't feel the need to drive the whole discussion, and they're happy — relieved even — to let me lead.

The third piece is the decision question. I said earlier that you and your prospect come to the sales call with really different goals. You want to sign up a client, and they want free information. We need to negate those opposing forces, and we do that with the decision question. I ask them, "Why now? Why me?" Those two questions get them telling you why they need help right now, and why they think you might just be the person to help them.

Next, we stretch the gap. We've talked about this in detail already. What are the results they want? What is their current reality? What are the road blocks holding them back? (Those are steps four, five, and six.) In each of these steps, we go wide, we go deep, we repeat back what they tell us, and we ask, "Is there anything else?" That's how we stretch the gap. We want them to get it intellectually and feel it emotionally, and that gets them ready to do something with you.

Our job in this whole process is to help them make a decision for themselves and for their future. Whether that involves you or not is completely up to them, and frankly it's not really any of your business, until they ask for your help. At the end of your conversation, they'll say, "Yeah, I'd like some help," or they won't. Simple, right? There's no weirdness, just "Are we a match, or not?"

So the last step is getting hired. In this step, we do three things: We check in for value, recap everything they've told us so far, and ask them if we've missed anything. I say, "Have I missed anything?" They usually say, "Nope." I ask them, "What's been most valuable so far?" They'll tell you what's been best about this conversation. Usually, what has been most valuable to them is the fact that they've been able to get it all out on the table. Finally, there's one person who totally gets them; who understands where they are and where they want to go. Plus, they're secretly hoping that person, you, can help them get the outcome they want.

You have to be really careful here. I have a rule: I don't go beyond this point unless I've already decided I want them as a client, unless I know I can help, and that I want to work with them. If you take the next two steps, there's a really big chance they'll give you money and want to work with you, whether you can help them or not. It's on you to make sure that you only do these last two steps if you've got the goods and can help them.

Next up is the three-question loop. Is this making sense so far? Are you comfortable with everything so far? Where do you think we should go from here? Here's where we dispense our six magic pills, one at a time, in combination with the three-question loop.

The Strategy Session Kit

The tool we use for this process with potential clients, with prospects, is the Strategy Session Kit. The first page walks you through results, reality, and roadblocks, with the six magic pills at the bottom. On the back is where you take your new client's details: contact information, program payments, their 12-month goals, and their 90-day progress. They go straight from making the commitment, past any decision anxiety, to getting excited about what comes next, about their 12-month goals and their 90-day progress.

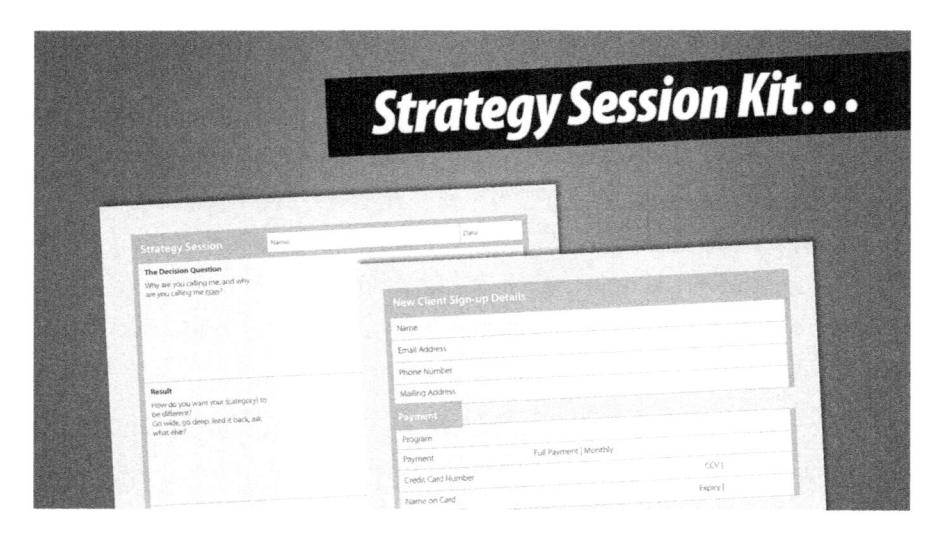

You can download The Strategy Session worksheets from www.MillionDollarCoach.com/kit.

Let's just pause and check in. What has been most helpful for you so far? I'd love to know.

Is this a coaching process vs. a consultant approach? What you do with a client after you sign them up is completely up to you. The sales process is identical. I've got a ton of consultants, a ton of coaches from around the world, in all sorts of different industries. Probably 80% are in the business-to-business space. Heaps of them in relationships, in health, in spirituality, in all sorts of different places. What you do with a client when you sign them up is up to you, but the marketing and the sales process is identical for coaches and consultants. If your question is, "Is the sales process more like coaching or more like consulting?" I'd say, it is more like coaching. The last piece, the six magic pills, is more like consulting, where you teach them what to do.

If you're coming to the live training Million Dollar Coach Intensive with me, then yes, we'll go into lots more detail about this at the live event. This book is like an overview, and the live event is more than a dive. Check out www.milliondollarcoachintensive.com.

Alistar says, *Hell yeah, MDCI was awesome.* Divia says, *Such great value, it was fantastic. It was great; I came out from Melbourne.* Joe says, *It was fan-freakin-tastic.* Eric says, *It is terrific.* Kevin says, *It is insanely good,* and he's added five exclamation marks. Tony says, *Exactly. All killer, no filler.* Karen says, *I am booked in, it is going to be great. Insanely good, enough fodder for a year. Totally,* Mark says, *insanely good, I keep telling you to charge more for it.* You totally do. *MDCI, ridiculously valuable,* says Harry. Trevor says, *I went to one in Santa Monica, California and one in Sydney, Australia. Flew all the way down. It was amazing. So amazingly good I can say it was worth the trip from Toronto to Sydney.* That's awesome. Rebecca says, *MDCI value sky high.* John says, *Compelling. Maybe exactly what I needed was the feeling I got from being there.* Ellen says, *It's the best program you can go to if you have a coaching business and you want to grow. It will resonate with your experience, give you words to express what is wrong, and show you exactly how to fix it.* Love that, right?

What has been most helpful so far? *Loving the six magic pills, feels clear.* Nick says, *I used to sell vacuum cleaners and asking, "Would you like this in red or black?" made me feel dirty.* Nothing worse than selling cleaning products and feeling dirty! *Moving from a sales process to a conversation with prospective clients.* Yeah, makes life so much easier. *Funnel filter.* Love that.

How can we overcome the objection, "I need to think this through?" Mate, really straightforward. You only have conversations with people who need it right now. In the triage call, you ask them, is this a later thing or a sooner thing? If they say it's a later thing, you say, "Thanks, let's stay in touch." There's no point having conversations with 'later' buyers. You only want to talk to people who have a real problem right now. In step three of the strategy session again, we say "Why now and why me?" You don't get, "I need to think this through," because everyone is at the point where they need it right now.

Is the price of the product mentioned in the funnel filter or the strategy session? When is the first time price should be mentioned? You have a couple of options. I do it right at the end, in the last 10 minutes of the strategy session. We still close 94% of the people we chat with into clients. If you are a bit worried about that, then put it in your webinar up front. We'll talk about webinars in a little bit.

How do I handle price objections or other objections? Don't get them. Mate, it's really straightforward because you walk people through, step by step by step. You might get questions, in which case you answer and say, "Where do you think we should go from here?" They'll say they'd love to do it.

Johnathan says, *This is the most elegant sales process I have seen, so much better than the old school insert guru's name here approach to selling.* Johnathan, it totally is.

What do you do with people whom you decide you can't help? Honestly, the short answer is, usually I don't even let them through the triage call. I say, "I said right up front my job today was to work out if and how I can help you. You need this and this and this. Honestly, I don't think I am your guy, but that person over there could be really great for you." Give them the website and wish them well.

Could you say more about the prescriptions? Totally. You are going to have to identify three core problems that they have and the prescription for each problem. For each problem, there's a matching prescription. If they don't have enough leads right now and it's hurting their business because they can't grow, you'd say, "What you need is a lead generation system that brings you a steady, consistent flow of highly qualified leads; you need a nurture system that warms them up to the point where they're an 8, 9, or 10 in terms of how likely they are to give you money." That's our prescription; it's the why and the what, but not the how. Then you move on to prescription #2.

Chapter 5: Rock Events

All right, in this chapter we're going deep into events. I'm going to give you some strategies and techniques I guarantee you've never heard before. These are the strategies I teach inside **Black Belt**; they're the ninja moves that make live events rock.

There's some magic, some special sauce that only happens when you're live in a room with your people. You can really rock events and just have a great time — teaching amazing stuff, connecting with people, and having them kind of marinate in your thinking, your world view. Whether your event's 90 minutes, three hours, a day, or even two days long, I think you're going to find what I'm about to share with you really helpful.

Here's the thing: If you've got the right structure for running conversion events, you'll do really well. If you don't, it's going to get hard.

When I was seven or eight, I was down in Darling Harbour (a Sydney harbour-side precinct) with my dad and my stepmom. It was a beautiful summer day, I was holding my dad's hand, we were walking around the harbour, and there was a busker performing on the street. A huge crowd was watching, like hundreds of people, as the busker worked up to his big finale. He was encouraging people to clap and cheer and make a whole lot of noise. His big finale involved juggling, fire, a unicycle, and just a bunch of craziness. People went absolutely ballistic, cheering and clapping, and I held my dad's hand and looked back over my shoulder at this busker when he called out to his crowd, "Don't clap; throw money!"

Don't clap; throw money.

Imagine you're at the front of your room. You're on stage and giving the audience your very best stuff. You've just delivered your big finale, and your audience is like, "Thanks, that was awesome!" They clap, and then they move on. They feel like they don't need to buy from you.

What you want to do instead is teach amazing stuff that leaves people hungry and thirsty for more — not just "boom!" and they're satisfied. If they say, "Thanks so much, that was amazing, you know, I think I can do this myself right now," that's a sign you're not doing it right. It's a sign you're delivering teaching content instead of *converting* content.

It happens to so many coaches and consultants when they do live events. At the end of the event they get applause, not money. They get feedback forms, not order forms. And when it's all over, they're exhausted. Live events can be a ton of work, and they just don't have a whole lot to show for it. That's what happens if you get this wrong, if you don't have a structure for selling.

When you get this right, here's what happens. You still deliver your best stuff. You drop value bomb after value bomb. You give away amazing stuff and people say, "That was incredible, I can't believe I got this much value from you."

When people come to my **Million Dollar Coach Intensive**, they think it can't possibly be any good because the price is so low. But MDCI is insanely good. It's value bomb after value bomb. Two whole days of "all killer, no filler".

Go ahead, teach your best stuff. Give your best stuff away, but give it away *the right way*. That's what makes a difference.

When you get to the close, the offer at the end, instead of being clunky and kind of awkward — or worse, weird and douchey — it's smooth as butter, it flows gracefully, and it's respectful. It builds desire instead of building pressure. At the end, instead of clapping, they throw money. They apply to work with you.

I was talking to a client the other day about a live event we built together, a conversion event designed to teach great stuff and sell his program. He was running the event on the weekend, and I spoke to him on the Friday before. I said, "What's your plan for the weekend?" He said, "I'm off to round up some clients," like he was a cowboy out lassoing cattle.

I've got to round myself up some clients! That's how this works.

Adam and Tristan

We have Black Belt clients who fill big rooms with hundreds and hundreds of people at their events. But you don't need big rooms; this works with smaller groups, too. In the last chapter, I mentioned Adam. He ran a workshop once with just eight people in the audience. Can you imagine just you and eight guys in a room? At the end of his presentation, he made his offer using exactly the same structure we're going to talk about in a moment. Of the eight people in the room, how many do you think bought? If two people took him up on his offer, he'd have had a conversion rate of 25%, right? If he had got four buyers, his conversion rate would have been 50%. Well, Adam didn't get two or four, or even eight; he sold thirteen out of eight. That's insane! What kind of conversion rate is that? 160%?

You can do incredibly well when you do this right, and we have heaps of clients now who are doing it well.

Tristan (whom I talked about earlier too) ran a live event in San Francisco. Again, there were small numbers: 30 people in the room. He sold 11 clients at $18,000 each — that's $198,000 dollars from one event.

So how do these guys do so well?

They do so well because they know how to structure a presentation for selling, not just for teaching. The structure is really different for a webinar or a workshop that sells.

What I want to know right now is, what do you find hardest about selling at events? If you've done it before, write down what you found hardest, and if you've never done it before, but you're thinking about doing it, what do you think the biggest challenge is going to be for you? What is the hardest part about selling at an event for you?

How to do the transition at the end. Kevin says, *Believing in the value.* Julia says, *I can sell at a 90-minute event, but I find it hard to sell at a one-day event.* It depends on what your offer is, right? Knowing the right thing to say and how to make it happen.

Feeling like you're trying to convince people to buy. If you can remember, we talked about auditioning versus impressing clients. *Scared about doing it. Call to action. Conversion. Need a good framework that works.* Yeah, you totally do. *The clap: They get heaps of value and they want to be my mate on LinkedIn, but they don't buy.* Matt, I hear you. *The close. Hardest thing is all the work and not enough conversions.*

Mel says, *It's hard if I think about it as selling, rather than serving.* Interesting distinction. *Transitioning from seminar to selling.* Here is the big idea, mate. The fact that you're thinking it's seminar here and selling there; that's the problem right there. It's not seminar, then sell; it's seminar and sell the whole way through.

Having an irresistible offer, says Steve. Great to have you here, man. Long time, no see. Coop says, *The transition. Feeling icky and making a really poor offer. Giving away too much or not enough content, not striking the right balance.* Right, but remember, it's not how much you give away, it's the way you give it away.

Own The Room

From the moment your potential client steps into your workshop room to the moment you step on stage, a game starts playing out. What happens in the first 30 seconds, the first two minutes, the first five minutes of your workshop, decides what's going to happen at the end.

You know the game Simon Says, which you played as a kid? When I say do something, you do it. That's how Simon Says works. The moment I step on stage, I say, "Do me a favour. Raise your right hand." I give them a moment to raise their hands. "Awesome. Now wave it around like you just don't care." Everyone waves their hands around like they just don't care. Then I say, "OK, put your hand on the shoulder of the person next to you. Give him a shake and say, 'Oh crap, he's interactive!'"

What just happened? I asked you to do five things. You did five things, and it went really well. I instructed, and you responded. I just owned the room.

In the first three to five minutes of a live event, you need to do these three things. You need to get their attention, create a connection, and get their permission. Once you've got their attention, got people's eyeballs hooked, and got them feeling like they're in the right place at the right time and that this event's going to be fantastic, you want to create a connection with them. That's why I get them to put their hand on the shoulder of the person next to them and give it a shake. Right from the start, we're in this together. It's an "us" room, not a "he and us" room. Do you know what I mean? You need to find a way to create a connection between you and them, and between them and each other.

After we've got their attention and created a connection, we need to get permission. You need permission for three things. First, you need permission for your style. Have you ever watched someone speaking, and they're teaching you really good, important stuff, but there's something about the way they speak, or the way they dress, or their manner, that just bugs you? You're trying really hard to pay attention, but you can't, because you're too busy sort of subconsciously judging them or counting the number of "um's" they say, or their shoes don't match their outfit, or their hair is messy. I do it all the time, it's actually embarrassing. The truth is, everyone does it, so it's best to get permission for your own idiosyncrasies right up front.

If you're a certain way, get permission for being that way. I was on Periscope yesterday and somebody said, "You talk too fast for me." I said, "Mate, if that's going to be a problem for you, I'm afraid we're not a good match. I'm going to talk quickly and with an Australian accent every time we talk. Right?" If we're not a match, let's have it out right now.

So you're going to get permission for your style: "Here's how it's going to roll today. It's going to be interactive. It's going to be fast.

It's going to be ..." You get the idea? Just get them ready for how it's going to work. "I'm going to teach for little bit, then we'll take questions for a bit."

You're going to get permission for your content, too. Say, "Here's what we're going to cover ..." Go through what you're going to cover in your talk and why it matters.

And thirdly, you're going to get permission for the sale at the end, to make them an offer. A great friend of mine, Kerwin Rae, says, "I suppose you're wondering if this is one of those talks where I give you a bunch of really great content, and then I am going to pitch you some high-priced, expensive product. Well, you don't have to worry: I won't disappoint you." That's hilarious; it's very Kerwin, but it's not my style. All you have to say is, "I am going to give you everything I can in the time we've got together, and at the end I'll show you where to go to get more help if you want it, is that okay?" They say, "Sure" — they always do — and now you've got permission to make them your offer at the end. They're actually expecting you to make them an offer.

So the first key is to **own the room**. It's your territory, so mark it. Play Simon Says. Have them know whose room this is. When I was in a room with Brad Sugars years ago, he asked the audience a question and nobody responded. There was just silence. Brad got all indignant; he breathed in, he paused, he took another breath and walked straight up to the front of the stage, eyeballing everybody. It got really intense. He said to everyone, "Since when was it okay not to participate in my room?" That's the posture I'm talking about.

Own the room. People want to be led, so lead them.

Install Influence

Somebody told me once that they loved "doing the seminar piece but when I get to the sale at the end, it gets weird."

That's what happens when you think about the seminar piece and the selling piece as two separate things. Your job is to design amazing content. Killer content, the best you've got. And then you're going to give it away, but you're going to give it away in a particular way, a way that has people wanting more from you.

You do that by *installing influence* all through your presentation.

Before we can install influence, you have to figure out what the influence is going to be, and here's how to work it out.

Get yourself six sets of Post-it notes (six different colours). On the first set of Post-it notes, write down the content topics you're going to talk about. What are the main topic areas? Maybe you're teaching online marketing, lead generation, and landing pages, or you're teaching dating, about how to meet and connect, and attract dates. Whatever it is you're teaching, list out the main topics.

On the second set of Post-it notes, list out all the objections someone might have for working with you: Maybe it costs too much. Maybe I don't have enough time, or my wife isn't supportive, or my husband won't let me spend the money. List out the objections you hear all the time, one per Post-it note.

Thirdly, think about your client stories: wins, testimonials, case studies. List them out, one per Post-it note.

Fourthly, outline the logistics of your program. (Remember magic pill #5 from the previous chapter?) How does your program or product work? Are there webinars, live events, or one-on-ones with you? List out the key logistical pieces, one per Post-it note.

Fifthly, who are the other people in your program who need to be positioned? Who are the team members your audience should know about (even if those team members aren't in the room)? Write down their names or their roles, one per Post-it note.

Finally, list out all the sexy pieces of gear that they can only get if they're with you, if they join your program. List out each of your cool tools, one per Post-it note.

Now, find a clear space on a wall and stick the main content areas, the topics, in a row across the top. Here's a real-life example from one of our Black Belt workshops:

Underneath the topic areas, put in the content, what you want to teach. What exercises do you want them to do? Do you have a story of someone who did really well with that piece? Put that Post-it note in there. Before that person started with me, what objections did they have? Say, for example, it was, "This program costs too much." Great, so stick that next to it. What tools did they use? Stick that Post-it on there, too.

For each piece of content, you're going to teach your heart out — and while you're teaching, you're going to make sure you tell those stories, show how it's worked for others, raise and answer the objections they had on the way. This way, the whole thing is teaching and the whole thing is selling. It's not teach, then sell; it's teach *and* sell. Let me show you what I mean.

TEACH ..*then*..> SELL

INSTALL INFLUENCE—TEACH AND SELL ALL THE WAY THROUGH.

Most people teach, and then they try to sell. They deliver a great presentation, then they try to retrofit an offer on the back. They feel like they're two different people: an expert and a sales person. They say, "When I am teaching, I feel amazing, and when I am selling, I feel icky." That's just weird and awkward, and it's no way to run a business.

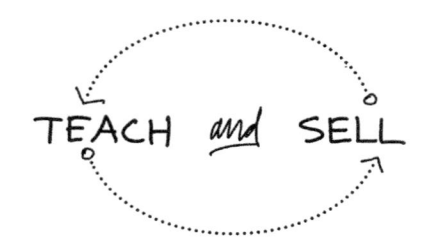

TEACH and SELL

INSTALL INFLUENCE-TEACH AND SELL ALL THE WAY THROUGH.

What we're going to do instead is install influence pieces all through our content. When you get to the offer at the end, it's easy because there's no extra sales bit to tack on. The whole workshop is teaching and the whole workshop is sales. Now when you're teaching, you're teaching people new information, and you're also teaching them what to want.

> What would happen to you if you taught the world's most amazing content and it made people hungrier to do more with you? Take a minute and write down what would happen for you, what would happen for your business, if you were able to teach and sell this effortlessly?
>
> *I'd own the room like a boss.* Wow — great stuff. *Coaching world domination! I'd be way more relaxed. I would be in full integrity, being*

my bad-ass self. Exactly, Brian. *They'd sell themselves.* That's exactly what happens. *I could make a great living doing what I love.* Mandy says, *It would be awesome!* Sharon says, *I would be out front finally. Pre-enrolled clients writing the offer.* Yes. Anton said, *I'd be authentic.* Bill said, *Selling could actually be fun. I would be satisfied and relaxed and do way better. Business would blast off,* says John. *Teach and sell is how I got to the 1% of 140,000 reps in my financial planning career in the US.* Matt, that's bad ass. *More conversion, more impact, more money.*

Choreograph the Close

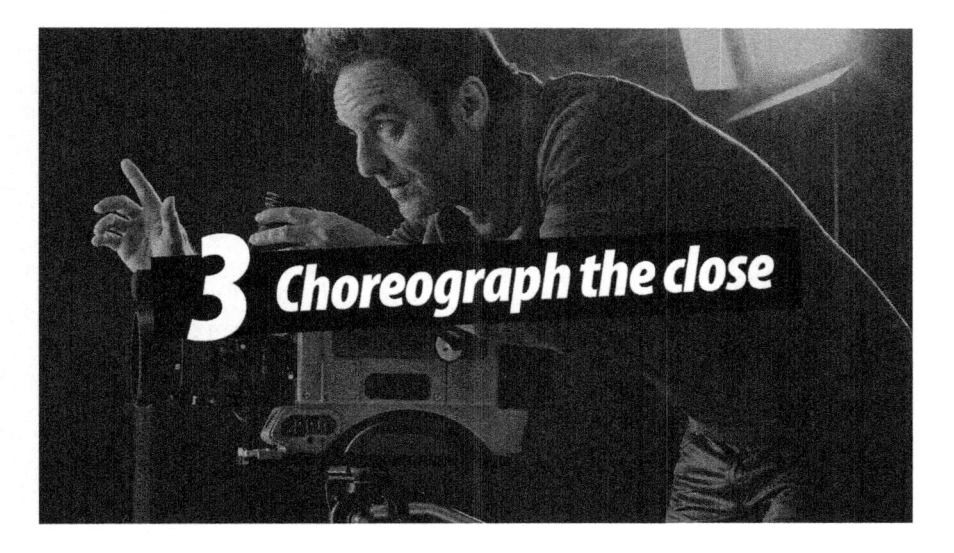

We've been talking about setting up the close, so it's easy. Now I'm going to show you how to choreograph the close itself so it's buttery smooth. Lead your audience through these four phases, and you'll build anticipation. You'll close out your workshop gracefully and elegantly.

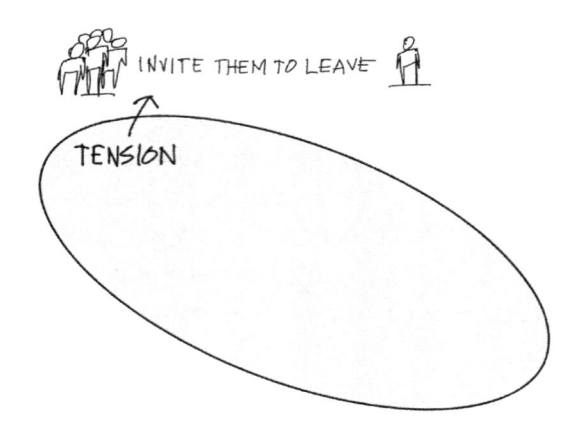

CHOREOGRAPH YOUR CLOSE-LEAD THE AUDIENCE THROUGH THESE 4 PHASES.

The first phase is **tension**. The big danger when you teach your heart out is that people say, "Thanks, that was amazing," and they think they can do everything themselves and don't need your help. We need to insert a piece of content, a piece of workshop, that gets people back in the "I really need help with this" frame of mind.

There are a bunch of different ways you can do that. The simplest way is just explaining the problem to them, making it really clear that if they walk out the door right now, there's no way they can make this work on their own. Your job is to create some tension, a bit like stretching the gap.

A great way to create tension in a group is to challenge them to choose whether they want to hear your offer or not. In other words, don't just make your pitch to everybody all at once.

I say something like, "Great, if you want to hear how this thing works, I'm really happy to have a low-key, casual conversation about it — if you don't, that's totally cool."

Then I take the opportunity to ask everyone to leave the room — go to the toilet, get a drink, whatever — then I say, "If you want to hear more about how it works, we'll see you back here in 10 minutes and

I'll take you through it." Really simple. I give people an out. More importantly, they choose an in.

That's how I do it, and it's worked really well. Over the last three years, 30%–40% of the people who come to the Million Dollar Coach Intensive become clients.

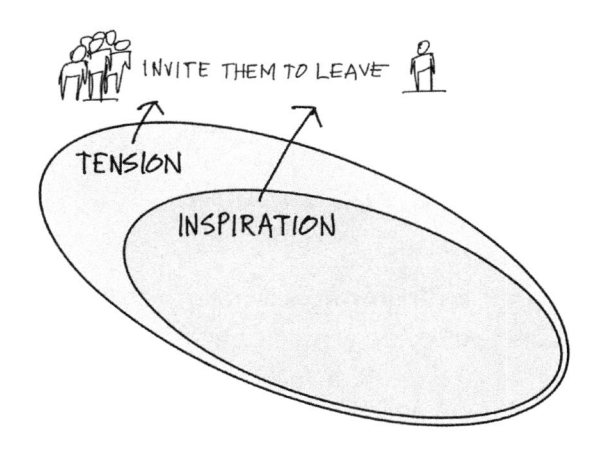

CHOREOGRAPH YOUR CLOSE-LEAD THE AUDIENCE THROUGH THESE 4 PHASES.

The second phase is **inspiration**. This is where you talk about the problem you solve and the promise you make. Talk about the cool people who are going to be there, how it works, and what your model is. You're walking them through the first four of the six magic pills, and your job here is to get people inspired, to get them excited about the opportunity.

Again, give people a chance to leave the room if they decide your program isn't right for them. I say, "Stay with us if you want to hear the details about how this works. If you don't, no hard feelings; feel free to go." I give people another out. Every time someone chooses to stay in the room, they're even more interested, more committed to the next step. What comes next? The walk-through.

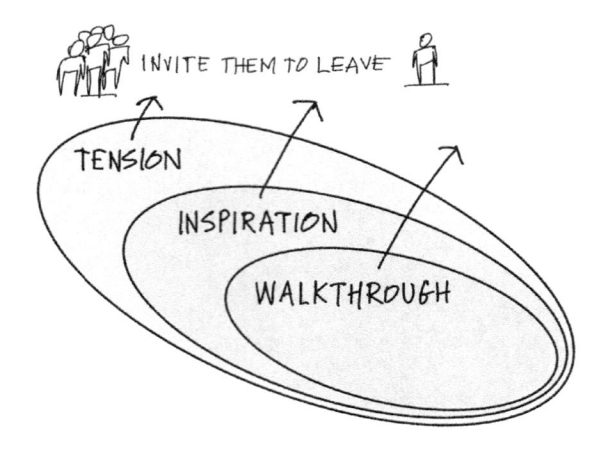

CHOREOGRAPH YOUR CLOSE-LEAD THE AUDIENCE THROUGH THESE 4 PHASES.

The third phase is the **walk-through**, where you take them through the logistics of how your thing works. Obviously, you need to do logistics in a sexy way; you can't just go, "Here's a big list of everything you'll get." That's boring. Package your logistics up into three core buckets that every single prospect needs (except for price; we'll come to that soon).

Just before the walk-through, I say, "Before we jump into this, I'd like to hear from two or three people. What is it about **Black Belt** that makes you know this is what you want to do?" Two or three people share why they want to join the program, and then I say, "Great, let me tell you how it works."

"In a minute, I am going to talk about price, but only with people who see the value, so if you don't see it, I'm going to give you one more chance to leave right now," and I give people another chance to opt out. By the time we get to the end, everybody's ready for the invitation.

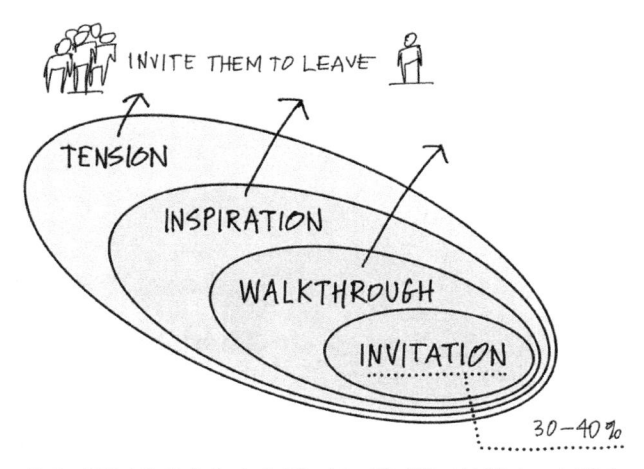

CHOREOGRAPH YOUR CLOSE-LEAD THE AUDIENCE THROUGH THESE 4 PHASES.

The **invitation** is when I talk to people about price and offer them a chance to buy. Here's what happens: 30-40% of people in my MDCI audiences apply to join the program. We don't accept them all: We reject about 30% of those applicants. We refund their deposits and walk away as friends. (That 30-40%, by the way, is of all the people who were in the room at the beginning, not just 30-40% of the people who are left at the end.)

The Influence Installer

Use the **Influence Installer** worksheet to map out your audience's beliefs and areas of resistance, and to work out which pieces of content you'll use to influence them.

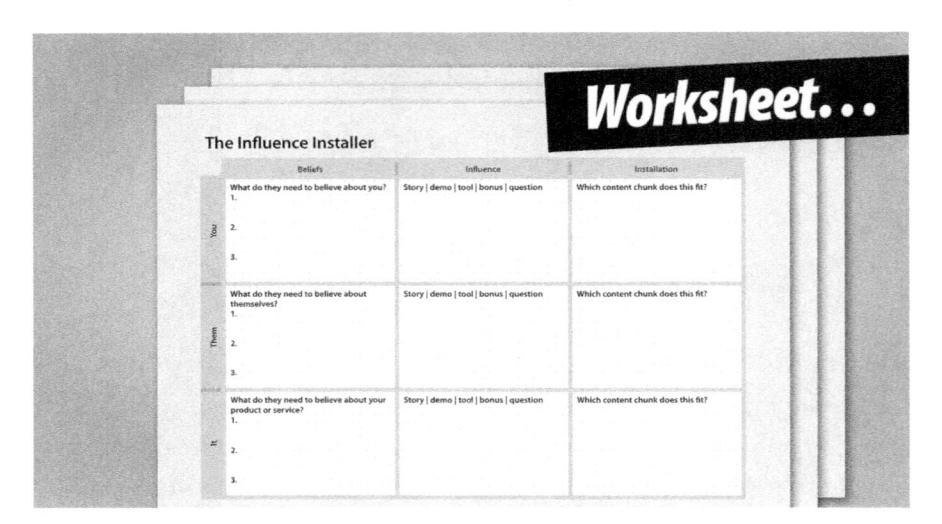

You can download the Influence Installer worksheet from www.MillionDollarCoach.com/kit.

> We've been talking about live events - what did you learn? What did you notice? Wendy says, *It works, I did it, you're a legend.* Shemal says, *Of the 30-40%, how many convert?* No mate, 30-40% of the people in the room convert. That's what I am saying. Coop says, *Best business decision ever joining* **Black Belt**. Legend. *Really sensible. Really easy to follow.*

*Where is this in the **Black Belt** member site?* Louise, go to the Event Marketing Intensive, Day 2, it's all in there. You can also check out the Influence Installer worksheet and the Choreograph the Close worksheet; they will step you through the process and the close in detail.

Teach and sell all the way through, says Pat. *Best close ever, they can opt out or in at any stage, so you filter down to the very best prospects.* Yes. *Love the Post-it note idea to organise the event.* Yeah man, that works so well. *Sales not separate to the conversion.* Yes. *Teach and sell the whole way through.* Trevor, message me inside the Facebook group and I will tell you what our three core buckets are. *Choreographed close is awesome.* Yes. *Super choreographed close,* love that.

When do you use the influence installer? Every moment that you teach your stuff. Steve, every piece of content that you teach has those pieces of influence in them. When I teach, whatever the topic is, I'm able to tell a client case study, raise and handle an objection, and share a win. Is this making sense?

Do I actually wait for them to leave the room? 100%. In fact, at the first opt-out, I make every single person leave the room. Only the people who want more are allowed back in after five minutes. So yes, they absolutely leave the room. Thanks for clarifying. There's no point pitching to people who don't want to hear it, mate. Mike says, *I had 23 people at my event,* by the way Mike's a client so that's his job, *I had 23 people at my event; $118,000 using the system,* legend. Perfect, man.

Chapter 6: Sell Webinars

In the last chapter, we talked about live events. Now, let's look at webinars. Webinars have the potential to be absolutely awesome for you, provided you have a great system for running them.

If you don't have good systems for your webinars, things go horribly wrong. For starters, running a webinar is an awkward thing to do. You're just sitting there at your place, on your own, talking to your computer. You can't see your audience, so there's no body language to read, no energy to feel — there's no feedback at all (unless you have a chat box running and you watch it like a hawk).

There's nothing worse than talking to people and they don't talk back. You're having a conversation with them and you ask a question and ... nothing, nobody responds. It's just awkward. If you don't have a good system, not just for creating great content, but creating great engagement on the call, your audience will sit back like they're watching TV, and you're the one left doing all the work.

Then, when it comes to the call to action at the end, you're hoping people will jump on your offer; you invite them to take the next step, and it's just you waiting there on your own. It's like being stood up on a date.

What you want instead is a bulletproof system, so you can deliver epic content. You want your webinars to be dynamic and engaging so you and your audience can have fun while they're picking up what you're putting down. When you ask a question, they all reply like a Southern Baptist revival church with the Reverend James Brown in charge. He sings out to his people, and they respond in raptures.

Here's my goal. On every webinar I do, I want my audience to say, "That was amazing, but where can I get some more?" At the end of your sales webinar, you want to create a stampede. You want them rushing for the order form, to sign up for the program, to book in for the triage call, or to purchase the package.

What I want to know is, why do you want to run a webinar that rocks hard and converts like crazy? I am going to look into the question box and check your answers. Thomas said he thought my tumbleweed impression was my Darth Vader voice. I found your lack of faith disturbing, Thomas. That is my Darth Vader. *I want to leverage my time. I want to impact more people. I want to scale. I want to be one of many and have more fun. To get value and convert. Rocket is what it is all about.* Kevin, Amen to that. *I don't want to have to leave my office. Give me more authority, more sales. I want to go to webinar, event, to big ticket package.* Denny, awesome. Totally can. Heaps of clients do it all the time. *I want to have fun and get results.*

I want to serve as many people as I can. Find some new friends because it is heaps of fun and I make money. I am sick and tired of all the work that goes into a traditional launch. Mate, I don't do launches. Maybe at some stage in the future we will, but I love evergreen. There is so much pressure on you if you do a launch. How much pressure is there on you to get it 100% right? If any one thing goes *boom,* that is that opportunity for the year to make sales. It is just mental, why would you close your shop every day of the year except one week? That is completely insane. That is not a business; that is a promotion.

Alistair says, *I've got some smoother language if it helps. It is funny to try and hear Aussies try to be American.* I agree. I suck at American, but I am having a good time and hopefully you are too. Alistair says, *Like a Southern Baptist revival.* That is what we're after.

Lars

I want to introduce you to a client of mine named Lars. Lars coaches real estate agents across the United States. He has an incredibly successful real estate business himself, he's at the top of his field in terms of sales volume and deals, and what's even cooler than that, is the fact that he's doing those numbers on two hours a week. Epic, right? When I met him, he'd started coaching other real estate agents, showing them how to do what he was doing. He was working one-on-one with about 20 clients, making about $40,000 a month. But it was all one-on-one sales and delivery.

We did three things. First, we tweaked his webinar. I showed him how to build a webinar that rocks hard and converts like crazy. We built the kind of perfect prospect pipeline we talked about earlier, and we built the kind of one-to-many delivery model we're going to talk about in the next section. We put all this together just over a year ago, and Lars has gone from $40,000 a month to $125,000 a month, gunning for $200,000 a month. He's on this path to epic scale, a massive trajectory. Why? It all started with webinars that rock.

There are three keys to building a webinar like this. (By the way, if you've been around me a while, you may have seen some earlier videos of me teaching webinars. I want to teach you a new, different, better way.)

Reverse Engineer It

The first key to building a webinar that rocks hard and converts like crazy is reverse engineering. Start building your webinar with the end in mind.

Here's the thing I want you to get. There are six steps to webinars that sell. (There's a different structure for webinars that teach content, but here we're focusing on webinars for selling.)

The opening, the first three to five minutes, is where you create attention, connection, and get permission. You get people in, excited, and hooked till the end. Everyone who joins a webinar is one click away from the bail button. They're thinking, "I'll check this out, but if it sucks, I'm gone." That's fair; that's what I'd do. That's what you'd do, too. We need to get them hooked and excited about staying to the end.

The second piece is the 'stick'. How do we get people to stick around until the 45-minute mark, where your offer is?

Thirdly, we have the stretch. The stretch is where we teach the content that makes people want what you've got. (We talked about stretching in our last chapter when we discussed installing influence, and the chapter before, auditioning clients. It's the same idea.) There are usually three modules of content in a good sales webinar, and when you build each one of these pieces, you install some influence.

Every piece of content you deliver needs to answer four questions positively:

1. Does it keep people engaged?
2. Does it give me a chance to show proof?
3. Does it set up the sale?
4. Will it be perceived as valuable content?

If you answer 'yes' to all four questions, you're building conversion content. So we've got the opening, stick, and stretch. Next, we need to *transition*, which is just another way of saying we need to go smoothly from the formal content part of the webinar to the part where I'm about to invite you to buy my stuff.

Then we have the offer itself, and after that we have the party, which is where we welcome new people to our program, the buyers. We tell them what's going to happen next, get them really excited about it, and then we have a Q&A session. The party is designed to welcome the new people, to make them feel great, and to help everyone else know that they're missing out, that the train is leaving the station soon, and they had better jump on it right now.

The last thing you do is run a short Q&A session for the people who aren't sure yet, and are thinking, "I really want to do this, but I have some questions."

PLAN

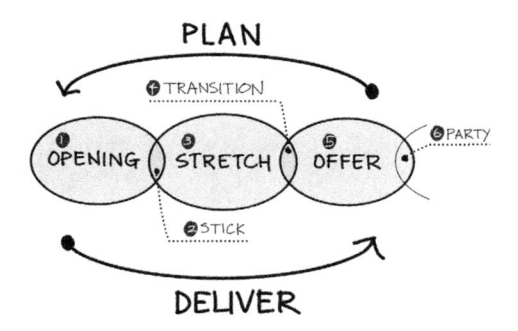

① OPENING ③ STRETCH ⑤ OFFER
④ TRANSITION ⑥ PARTY
② STICK

DELIVER

REVERSE ENGINEER YOUR WEBINAR—START WITH THE END IN MIND.

Those are the six steps for a webinar that sells, and that's the order we deliver them in: Opening, Stick, Stretch, Transition, Offer, Party. But when we plan the webinar, when we prepare, we do it backwards. We start with the offer and work back towards the opening. If you don't do it this way, you'll make the mistake that everyone makes: You'll have great content, and then you'll try to duct tape an offer onto the end, which just doesn't work.

Here's what you're going to do instead. Figure out what your offer is first. What's in it? What's it all about? What are its core components? Once you've got your offer figured out, you'll know what you need to teach in order to have people wanting it.

One of my gifts, I think, is teaching content in a way that creates action. When I'm working with clients, I teach them stuff, and they take action. That's why we get so many amazing results. When I'm selling, it's basically the same: I teach great stuff in a way that makes people go, "You know what, I really need this," and, like my clients, they take action right away — only, this time, the action is signing up for Black Belt.

So figure out your offer and say, "Great, that's the offer; what do I need to teach in order for people to want that?" And then craft each piece of content so it snowballs into an easy 'yes' at the end. Teaching them what to want is just reverse engineering.

Create Conversion Content

For this to work, we need great conversion content. This is a lot like installing influence, except we're doing it on a webinar instead of a live event. I said earlier that there are three pieces of content in a webinar that sells. Each of those pieces is about 10 to 15 minutes long. I'm going to teach you how to deliver them, so you're creating conversion content and not providing people with information.

THEME	SET SCENE	−/+
TEACH	PROOF	PERSONALISE
STRETCH QUESTION	LINE IN THE SAND	PROMISE

CREATE CONVERSION CONTENT—HOW TO DELIVER CONTENT THAT SELLS.

First, **decide on the theme** for this particular piece. For example, our theme for this piece of content is "running webinars".

Second, **set the scene**. You know when you're watching the first 30 seconds of a TV show, and they set up the story line? They're called 'establishing shots' in the industry. Usually, there's not much dialogue; they just show you where you are. They're setting the scene for the action.

To set the scene, imagine your prospect at the very moment they need you most. Where are they? What's happening? If we're talking about running sales webinars, our prospect is sitting in front of their computer; they've just finished their delivery. What's happening? Well, it didn't go very well. Cue crickets chirping, tumbleweeds blowing down the street. Who's there? It's just our prospect, no-one else. Their audience has left and there are no buyers. How are they feeling? I'm pretty sure you can imagine. Set the scene, paint a picture, and get people involved in the theme.

Next, **do a *why stack***. Call out three specific frustrations and the consequences that can happen if they get this wrong. Then, show them the alternative for each frustration. Show them what can happen when they get it right. Lay out the problems and the promise.

Then we teach the stuff. Show proof that it actually works: case studies, testimonials, statistics. Show them examples where they can see how it's worked for other people, and get them thinking it really could work for them too.

The next step is to **make it personally relevant**. Using our webinar theme as an example, I might say, "You've seen the six steps it takes to run a webinar, and you've seen how well it worked for Lars. Let's talk about you for a little bit. What would happen to you if you could run a sales webinar, and in 70 minutes you'd have 30 or 40 people saying yes to your offer? Whether it's buying a product, purchasing a ticket for an event, or booking in for a sales appointment, what would happen?" What did I just do? I asked a stretch question.

Now, we draw a line in the sand. I say, "Now you know. You can keep selling one-on-one, the old, slow, dumb, hard way, or you can run webinars that allow you to rock hard, deliver amazing results, wow people with your knowledge and skill, and leave them wanting more. So what's it going to be? Do you want to keep doing it the old way? Or is it time you mastered webinars?" Draw a line in the sand and make them choose.

Finally, relate everything back to the big promise at the start of the webinar. We'll do that three times, once for each of the three pieces of conversion content we deliver.

That's how you create conversion content. It's a content that doesn't just teach; it proves the stuff; it shows that it works. It teaches the theory, the why, the what, the human interest, and then it relates it back to them, and it has them make a decision like, "Holy crap, I need that!" When you deliver webinars like this, you're not just teaching them — you're teaching them what to want.

Deliver Workshops, Not Webinars

Here's the mindset I want you to have when you're delivering your webinars. Deliver workshops, not webinars. Deliver your webinar like you're James Brown in the pulpit at a southern Baptist revival meeting.

Think about it for a second: What makes a great workshop great? Great workshops are interactive. They're engaging. There's heaps of energy. There's heaps of learning. People get loads of value. They're practical, hands on. Run your webinars the same way.

In a webinar, there's nothing more awkward than standing in front of your computer and talking at the screen. There's nothing more boring than being the person on the other end of that screen hearing the presenter read out a list of bullet points. It sucks for you, and it sucks for them, too.

Here's how to make your webinars better for both of you. The secret is to think online workshop, not webinar. How do you turn it into an online workshop? You have great visuals. You tell great stories. You ask questions. You check in with people, and you read out their responses. For example, when people join your webinar, have a look down the list of who's on the line and say stuff like, "Hey Alex, so great to have you here. Alistair, thanks for your comment before! I really appreciate that; it was really helpful." Scroll down to the letter J and say, "Jonathan and Josh, thanks for being here. By the way, bunch of clients on the line, it is fantastic to have you here." Say where you are in the world right now. Engage people individually. If they ask a question, then answer it. Pause and tell a story. Draw a model on your iPad. If you make it a workshop instead of a webinar, it's way more fun for you, and way more fun for them, too. Engagement goes up. Involvement goes up, and without involvement there can be no commitment. Deliver workshops, not webinars.

We just talked about three keys for running a webinar that rocks. I want to know, what was most valuable for you? Was it reverse engineering and planning it backwards? Was it creating the conversion content? Or was it the workshops-not-webinars idea? Which one of those three was most helpful for you? Take a moment and write down your answer now.

Being able to hear other people's experience. Keeping it relevant and interactive. Step me forward. Conversion content. Workshops, not webinars. Yeah. *Reverse engineering it.* Perfect.

How to Build Your Webinar With The Pitchdeck Planner™

There are a couple of tools we use when we build sales webinars like this.

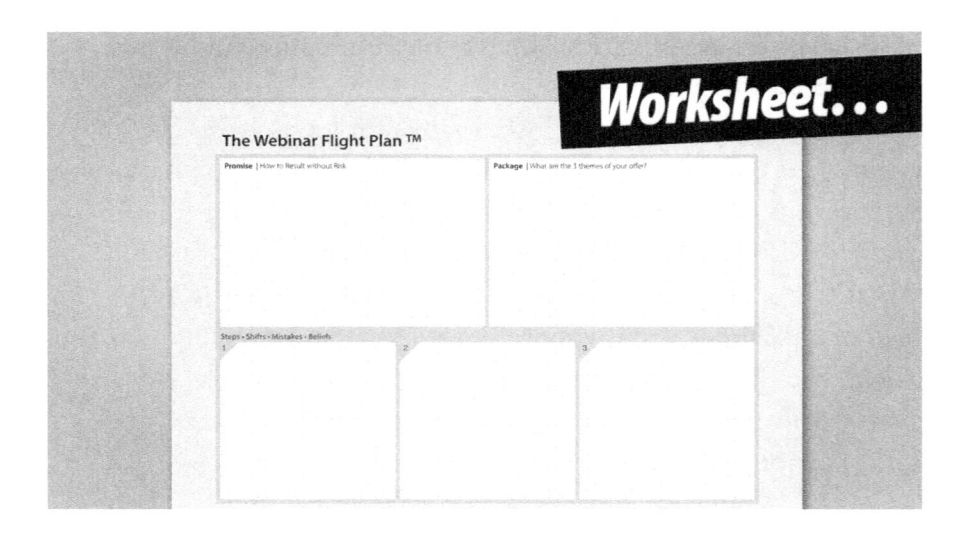

The first is called The Webinar Flight Plan. It helps us work out what the promise should be, what the title is, and what the three pieces of content should be.

When it comes to building your webinar, don't go straight to your computer. Plan it out on paper first. We storyboard the whole webinar on a gigantic worksheet called The Pitchdeck Planner. It's jumbo sized; we get them printed on A0-size paper, which is about the biggest piece of paper most printers can handle. It's enormous. Stick it up on your wall and literally sketch out your presentation with a Sharpie: The Opening, The Stick, The Stretch, all three of the Conversion Content sections, The Transition, The Offer, and The Party. Mapping it out on paper first makes building your Keynote or PowerPoint slides a whole lot easier.

You can download The Webinar Flight Plan and The Pitchdeck Planner from www.MillionDollarCoach.com/kit.

John says, *How do you keep your mind on the structure of the webinar and watching comments on the feedback?* That is such a good question. Here's the deal. When you have been doing it for a while, it's easy. The secret is flicking backwards and forwards. When I'm teaching, I'm looking here; I don't even care about the chat box which is down there. When you're doing your first few webinars, instead of flipping backwards and forwards, get a wing man. Someone to help you out. You can just teach the stuff, and they can manage the chat; that's the secret when you first get started.

Lyndsay says, *When you talk about install influence, what cool gear do you mean? Framework, IP, physical stuff?* I mean physical stuff. For example, I've shown you some worksheets today. If you'd like to get a copy of all the worksheets we mentioned today, you can download them all, The Pitchdeck Planner, The Flight Plan, all those things. If you'd like to get them, just type the word 'yes' in the chat box right now. You can't see my screen directly, but there are about 70-80 'yes' responses right now. What are these things? They're cool tools that people want. See what I mean? If I had something for sale right now, I'd say, "When you join my program, you get all these tools." Make sense?

Louie says, *That was awesome, thank you.* Taylor is saying, *What is good software for hosting a webinar?* Listen, there are heaps of different ones. The industry standard is called GoToWebinar; it's been around for years. It is a bit expensive though, and there are plenty of other good options on the web today.

How do you have people leave on a webinar like you do at live events? Wendy, that's a great question. I don't have to engineer it: If they're not into it, they'll just bail. Yeah? Matt says, *You make my head buzz so much I don't want to sit anymore.* Then stand, even when I'm delivering a webinar at home on my own I stand, it just makes your energy heaps better. *What is your program for folks in the launch phase?* Million Dollar Coach Implementation Program.

PART THREE

DELIVER

Chapter 7: Decide Model

The biggest problem most coaches have is the model they bought into when they started out. Whether you're a coach or a consultant, the traditional model goes something like this: knock on doors, collect cards, follow up manually, sell one-on-one, and start working with each client individually.

Don't get me wrong; you can get results this way — sometimes great results — but you're locked into a model that doesn't leave you very much freedom at all.

First, you see the same problems over and over again. I don't know about you, but I love variety. I want a business that keeps me fresh. A business that helps people who are just starting out with you to get the answers they need, without you having to regurgitate the same information multiple times.

I don't want to feel like I'm tied to the business, day in, day out. Remember Adam, our head coach? He runs our Million Dollar Coach Implementation Program (which helps people get to $10,000 a month really quickly.) When we were thinking about building this program, Adam said, "I really need to leverage this program; I've just been stuck in a one-to-one session with a client while my mate's been rushed off to hospital." They didn't know if Adam's friend was going to make it or not. Adam really wanted to be there for his friend, but he couldn't get to the hospital because of his work commitments.

If we'd built the Million Dollar Coach Implementation Program around a traditional, one-on-one delivery model, Adam would have had more commitments and much less flexibility. He'd have had even less time for his friends.

Time-for-money, one-on-one coaching puts a cap on three important things: the amount of income you can make, the degree of independence you have, and the difference you can make with your clients. If you're anything like me, you got into coaching for all those reasons, because you wanted to make a meaningful difference in people's lives.

Whenever you run a model that's built around your personal time and effort, there's only so much time available, and you can only put in so much effort. Those two factors put a lid on everything else. They keep you playing small — you're like a giant who thinks he's a midget. You're a big guy squeezing into a small room. You're helping half a dozen people, a dozen people, maybe twenty if you're busy, instead of helping hundreds, or even thousands of people. You might be making a big impact with that small group of people, but the rest of the world doesn't even know you exist. They'll never benefit from your knowledge or experience because you're completely invisible to them. It's time to stop playing small.

If you look at your business, look at how this year has gone so far, how last year went, maybe the year before that. I'm sure you've made some progress. Eventually, though, when you keep doing the same stuff year after year, you hit a ceiling. Then you say, "Man, maybe this is as good as it gets. Maybe I should just settle."

I just want to let you know right now: That's complete BS. If you keep the same model, that's definitely as good as it's going to get. You can get busier, you might make a bit more money, and you'll definitely get more tired.

If you want to do something that sets you free, now is the day to change things. Mate, this is straight from the heart. 'As good as it gets' is like your Game One. Game One was awesome — after all, it got you to this place — but Game One is only getting you ready for what's coming next.

The way to get to what's coming next is to change the way you deliver. Cool? Listen, here's what happens. Instead of dealing with the same problems all over again, instead of Groundhog Day, this lets you do your art.

This means heaps to me. I want to help you, and I hope that it also lands with you. Here's the deal. About a year and a half ago, I took a step back and looked over everything that was happening in the business. I started wondering what would happen if I poured the same love, care, and attention I was pouring into the visual side of my business — my slide decks, my workbooks, all the things we present to our clients — what if I poured all that love into the rest of my business, too?

What if I could pour my heart and soul, my passion, into everything we do? And that's how we grew this incredible customer service; it's why we obsess over the first 100 days of a new client. We do all this stuff because we're 'arting' our business. It's like I've got a little corner of the world where I can pour my heart and soul into making everything we touch a little bit extraordinary.

I'm inviting you to do the same thing. What if — instead of just groundhogging it — you could build something extraordinary in your corner of the world too? How amazing would that be? All these extraordinary little corners all over the world.

When Steve Jobs was courting John Sculley to come and work at Apple, Sculley was head of marketing at Pepsi Co. Jobs had been trying to get Sculley to come and work with him for years, but Sculley had a good thing going. He had a great job at one of the biggest companies in the world, he was set for life, and in the end it came down to this. Jobs eyeballs Sculley, so the story goes, and he says, "Do you want to spend the rest of your life selling sugar water? Or do you want to come with me and have a chance to change the world?"

This is your chance to change the world.

> We've been talking about why it matters to me to build a leverage model. What I want to know for you is, why do you want to do this leverage thing? What out of what I've just said has resonated with you?

Replies: *Groundhog Day for me for seven years. Change the world.* Totally, freedom. More freedom, more choice. Reach more people and create my art. *I'm too lazy for people work.* He-man is on the phone. *Mate, freedom and catch up on the time and yes, to spend more time with my son. I want to play big.* Right? You get this. *Freaking time to play a freaking bigger game.* Exactly.

George

I want to introduce you to my client, George, from Seattle, Washington. George is a great guy; he and his business partner coach chiropractors around the States. He's just a legend of a man. When I first talked to him two-and-a-half years ago, they had 200 clients and called every one of those clients every two weeks, which means they were making, on average, 400 coaching calls a month.

Can you imagine making 400 coaching calls every month?

Back then, George told me, "I work six days a week. I wake up in the morning at 6:00 AM, pick up the phone, and coach through to 7:00 PM. I start with people in London, I follow the sun around the world, and I end the day coaching people in Hawaii. Only the client's in Hawaii and I'm stuck in my house!"

This is what George said, word for word, when I talked to him: "I wake up in the morning, I look at the phone, and I want to puke."

I met George at the Million Dollar Coach Intensive, and we mapped out a plan. Now, my coaching model has three core components: Attract, Convert, and Deliver. Which one do you do first? Well, you do whichever one is the biggest bottleneck for you. With George, there was no point helping with Attract or Convert because his biggest problem — by a mile — was Deliver.

So we mapped out a leveraged coaching program (exactly like we're about to do together). Getting people started in a leveraged coaching program is one thing, but now George had a different problem.

"What do I do with the 200 clients I've already got?"

George talked to each one of his clients, like he usually did. Except this time he had a 'transition conversation' with them, telling them why he built this new thing, and how it was a way for them to get bigger results even faster with one tenth the face time.

Here's what happened: All George's clients jumped on the new plan. This is just epic. He's gone from his old way — from six days a week, 6:00 AM to 7:00 PM, and wanting to puke every day — to one week on, one week off, all in the space of a month.

When I saw George at our next event, he said, "Mate, here's what I've done in the last 30 days. I've switched all my clients over to this new model, I work one week on, one week off, and I've freed up 26 weeks a year. I'm free!" That's amazing.

Closing $120,000 worth of business in your first webinar is pretty awesome. Freeing up those 26 weeks is even more awesome. George has heaps more time with his family and has started some new businesses — all because he moved to a coaching model that delivers money, freedom, and meaning.

Let me show you how to do it, too. Here are three things you need to know about building a business that fits you like a glove.

Fit Your Own Mask First

I'm sure you've been on a plane when the flight attendants do their safety demonstration, when they say, "If the cabin fills with smoke, an oxygen mask will drop from the unit above your head." Then what do they say next? They say, "Fit your own mask before assisting other passengers."

Just think for a moment, what would happen if you didn't do that? Let's say there's literally no oxygen in the plane, and you totally need a mask to breathe, but you decide to go all hero and help everybody else before you put your own mask on. How many people could you help before you pass out? Let's make it even easier for you; let's say you're in an aisle seat and you've got really good Harry Houdini breath-holding skills. How many people could you help then? Half a dozen people? Maybe 10 people?

Thomas says, "*If you keep your seat belt fastened, then it's two; you can only help the people either side of you.*" I love that — you've got the safety first going on, mate. I'm sure you're the guy with his tray table up-right and his window shade up too. Wendy says, *I used to work for an airline; I can tell you the answer is zero, you will help zero people.* Mel says, *"Hell, they're on their own. Save yourself!"* Right, that's what I'm saying — fit your own mask first!

Well, that's exactly how the average coach works. We're so busy fitting masks on everybody else, we forget to take care of our own mask first, and then we run out of oxygen. We burn out or we go broke. Whatever model you choose, make sure you're looking after yourself first. Make sure you're around long enough to bring your best to the people around you.

Set Your Mix

Building the perfect business model is a lot like a DJ or a sound engineer setting the controls on a mixing desk. See all those sliders?

Think of them like controls in your coaching business. There are 11 specific adjustments you can make to set your own perfect mix.

Let's run through a few of them. For each one, you get to decide, "Okay, here's the full range. I can go all the way down here at one end, or right up there at the other end, or I can be somewhere in the middle. Where do I want to be?"

For example, the first control on your business model mixing desk is the 'expert—host' control. Do you want to be the expert, the person with the original content? Or do you want to be a host like Oprah Winfrey, someone who brings in other experts? You don't need content of your own; you curate other people's content for your clients. That's completely cool; it's a great way to run a business. Maybe you'd prefer to be somewhere in the middle: You've got your own thing that you do, and you bring in other people, other experts when that makes sense. Me, I play expert. That's totally in my sweet spot. The question is, where do you want to be?

The next slider is 'specialist—generalist.' Do you want to be a specialist, focusing in on one specific niche? Or do you want to be a generalist, someone who takes general principles and applies to them in all sorts of different situations? Maybe you're somewhere in the middle, taking well-known general principles and applying them to your particular area. Maybe that's your thing.

What about the 'local' or 'global' slider? You could run your business in your local community only, or somewhere in the middle, like the west coast, or maybe you're national, or you could be all the way up the other end, working all over the world. Where do you see yourself?

You can choose if you want to deliver your stuff live, or if it's pre-recorded. You can choose whether you work online or offline. Do you want to help people short term with a specific result or long term in, say, a 12-month program that covers loads of ground? When people join, can they start any time or is there an intake?

Don't copy the tactics... Model the thinking.

You get the idea, right? When you're deciding your business model, don't just copy mine. That's the last thing you want to do. Choosing someone else's mix is a bit like wearing their underpants. Sounds kinky at first, but then it's just a little bit creepy, a bit weird. Those undies are never going to fit you quite right.

Set your own mix; build the business model that's perfect for you.

Work the 5 Ones

3 Work the 5 ones

I learned to **work the five ones** from a great friend of mine, Clay Collins, the guy who built LeadPages. It hit me right away: This is the fastest way to get to a million dollars a year. If you're already at a million a year or beyond, feel free to break these rules. If you're not there yet, and you're anywhere below $84,000 per month, then following this plan will get you there much, much faster.

Can you get there without working the five ones? Of course, but it'll be heaps slower. It'll take you much longer. Every time you break one of these rules, I reckon you multiply how long it takes to get results.

The quickest way to get the money you want is by working the five ones. What are they? I'll teach them to you in just a second, but here's what you need to know first: Building a million-dollar-a-year, scalable coaching business where you help more people, have more fun, and make more money is all about doing less, not adding more.

It's about pruning, not planting.

Think about your email inbox: Do you have enough emails? Of course you do. What about your to-do list: Have you got enough jobs? Of course you do. Right? Since when has the answer to 'too much' ever been 'more'? Since never. The answer has to be to simplify.

Here's what we're going to do: We're going to pare things back, ask five simple questions, and come up with one simple answer for each of those questions. We're going to work the five ones. Once you've made your decisions, that's it; they're the ones we're implementing. This is liberating when you get it. I'll admit it's also a little bit scary, and I'm totally cool with that. I'm happy to scare you if it results in an outcome.

You ready? Here we go, here are the five ones:

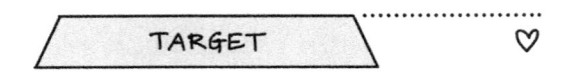

```
    ┌─────────────────────┐      ....................
   /      TARGET           \            ♡
  /_____\
```

WORK THE FIVE ONES—THE FASTEST WAY TO A MILLION DOLLAR BUSINESS.

The first one is **one target market,** i.e. one type of person you want to help. Specifically, I mean one person with one problem. Have you ever met someone who says, "I'm a marketing expert, but I've also got this multilevel vitamin company, and we can fix lawnmowers, too." What happens to their credibility? Zoom, goes through the floor. Trying to be all things for all people is stupid. Just because your coaching skills could help everyone, doesn't mean you should. Pick one target market, okay?

I can see people freaking out already. One target market. How do you know which target market to choose? You want to pick one target market that you love, that you just want to serve, that you want to give your all to. One target market, not five different audiences, or three, or even two. Uno. Got it?

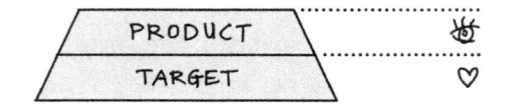

```
    ┌─────────────────────┐      ....................
    │      PRODUCT         │           👁
   /──────────────────────\      ....................
  /        TARGET          \           ♡
 /_____\
```

WORK THE FIVE ONES—THE FASTEST WAY TO A MILLION DOLLAR BUSINESS.

The second one is **one product**. Not five products, but one. Why just one product? Because you want to look a prospect in the eye and say, "This thing will get you the result you're after," and know — with absolute, unshakable, bulletproof confidence — that you'll get the outcome they're looking for.

Martin says, *I'm working with two starting products and have clients in both. Do I turn clients in one of them down?* Mate, what I would do is keep the clients you've currently got and focus on the product you want to grow. What you feed grows. Martin, sell the thing you want to sell. If money falls in your lap somewhere else, pick it up and collect until you don't need to anymore.

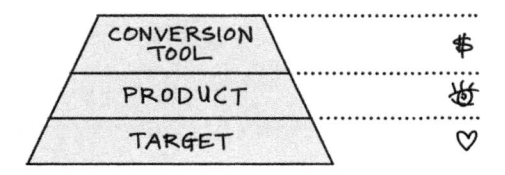

WORK THE FIVE ONES—THE FASTEST WAY TO A MILLION DOLLAR BUSINESS.

Next, we're going to build **one conversion tool**. In the previous section we talked about one-on-ones, webinars, and events. I gave you three options to choose from, and your job is to decide which one to build. Not all three, just one. One that consistently converts prospects into clients. (Once you hit a million dollars a year, feel free to change it. Until then, choosing one conversion tool will get you there faster.)

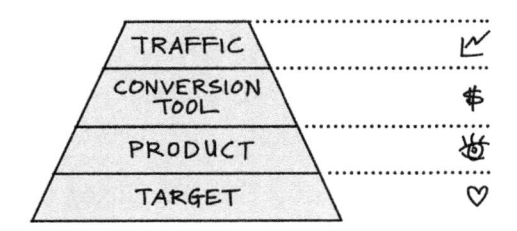

WORK THE FIVE ONES—THE FASTEST WAY TO A MILLION DOLLAR BUSINESS.

So far we have one product, one target, one conversion tool; next we need **one traffic source**. In the first section, we talked about free, paid, or partnership marketing. This is the same deal as before: Now you get to choose one of those sources. (Now, if you're choosing paid, that doesn't mean you can only use Facebook and can't do YouTube. They all count as paid.) Which one should you choose? Choose the one that's easiest for you to scale. Cool? One traffic source, easiest to scale.

Now we've got four ones: one target market, one product, one conversion tool, and one traffic source. There's one left.

If you wanted to grow a million-dollar-a-year coaching business quickly, what do you think the fifth one could be? Here's what it is: **one year**. You don't get to choose this one; it's just part of the rules for working the five ones.

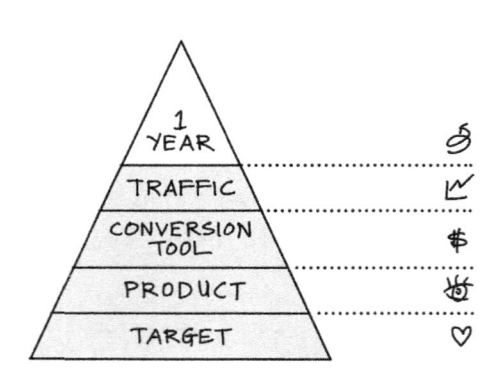

WORK THE FIVE ONES—THE FASTEST WAY TO A MILLION DOLLAR BUSINESS.

Why a year? Well, because here's the thing. It's going to take a year to get really good at these things. It's going to take consistent tweaking. What do most people do? They start something new, all excited, and when it doesn't work as well as they had hoped, they go and try something else. They never give themselves enough time to get good at anything.

Our job here with the one year is simple (though not always easy). You give yourself a year, so you can sharpen your skills and improve your results. It might take a few attempts. Maybe you'll smash your first webinar, maybe it'll take three or four before you hit your stride.

I still run webinars — they're a cornerstone of my marketing — and every time I run one, I find ways to improve. After each one, I do a quick debrief and make the next one better. Why? Because I'm always sharpening the blade.

Let's just think about the opposite for a moment. Let's say you do what most coaches do, and instead of working the five ones, you say, "I'm going to have four different target markets and three different products. I'm still going to do one-on-one, I'm still going to run webinars, and I'm still going to run events. I'll get traffic from networking and ads, and content marketing, and JVs."

What happens when you run a business like that? You get overloaded, you scatter yourself all over the place, and you burn out. And how good do you get at any of those things? Not very good.

Here's the plan instead: One target market, one product, one conversion tool, one traffic source, and we tweak them for a year until we're really, really good at them. How do you know which ones to pick? You get an expert who's done it a million times to help you. That's as simple a plan as it gets.

Choose smart, that's what we do. Work the five ones.

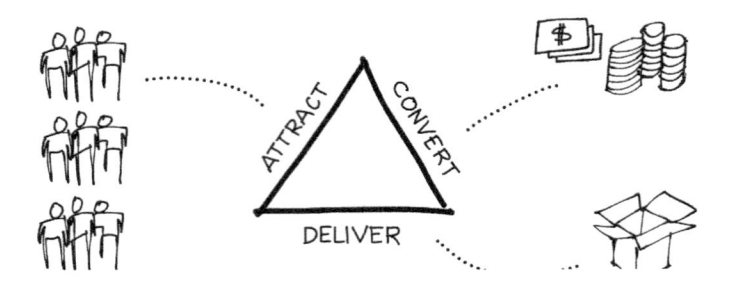

You've probably seen the model where people have something free. Then they have something cheap. Then they offer you something not so cheap. Then, there's this other model where you're supposed to sell something expensive. It's called an ascension model. Something really expensive, and then something OMG expensive. Everybody's seen this model. I think it's ridiculous. I think it's incredibly difficult for you to pull off and it overwhelms your client. I'd like to propose a much, much simpler model that falls in line with the five ones. It looks like this. This is what I want you to do.

Instead of having something little and free, we're going to build something extraordinary and free. Your free thing is going to be world-class good. Good enough that people would be happy to pay hundreds of thousands of dollars for it.

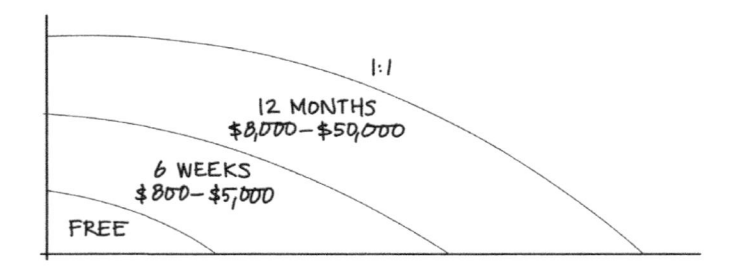

Next, I imagine there's a really good chance that many of you would like to have a small handful of one-on-one clients at a premium price somewhere at the top. That's cool, I think you should totally do that. So the question is, what goes in the middle? Well, your leverage program is going to have one of two offers. You get to choose which one of these two you want to do. You can have something short, say six weeks or so, or you can have something longer, like a 12-month program.

Now, let's talk about price points. Six-week courses are usually delivered online. A series of videos once a week and a Q&A is a really common format. The price point depends on your market and the return you're going to get from people. They usually start around $500. Yvonne Hill, one of our clients, sells her eight-week program for $8,000. So your short program will probably fall somewhere between $500 and $8,000.

You might be thinking, "So what's the difference between a $500 program and an $8,000 one?" Well, the main difference is asking for a higher price; it's understanding the cost of not hiring you, the cost of not getting the problems solved, and the value of the problem you're solving. If you're solving a $100,000 problem, then $8,000 sounds like a bargain.

Price points for 12-month programs also depend on your target market, but typically I sell the longer programs for between $8,000 and $50,000.

The question is, which model should you start with? Let me help you really quick. If you have a following already, have built courses before, and know you can sell your program, then go big. If you don't have a big following, haven't built stuff before, and don't know for sure that people are going to buy your program, then start with a six-week course.

All I want to do right now is ask you to make a choice: Are you going to sell something short, six to eight weeks, or something long, 12 months plus? What's it going to be? Take 15 seconds and write it down: short or long?

Short and snappy. Six weeks first. Long, 12 plus. Yeah. *Six weeks*, Love that. *Short, 12 weeks.* I don't know about 12, Rachel. If you can give me a really clear, obvious reason why it should be 12, okay, but I think for a specific result, short term, six to eight weeks is great.

Short. Yeah, most of us start with short. I think that's awesome. *Long.* Okay, good. Whatever you decided, that's perfect.

The Million Dollar Mixing Desk

Here's the worksheet we use for deciding your business model, called The Million Dollar Mixing Desk.

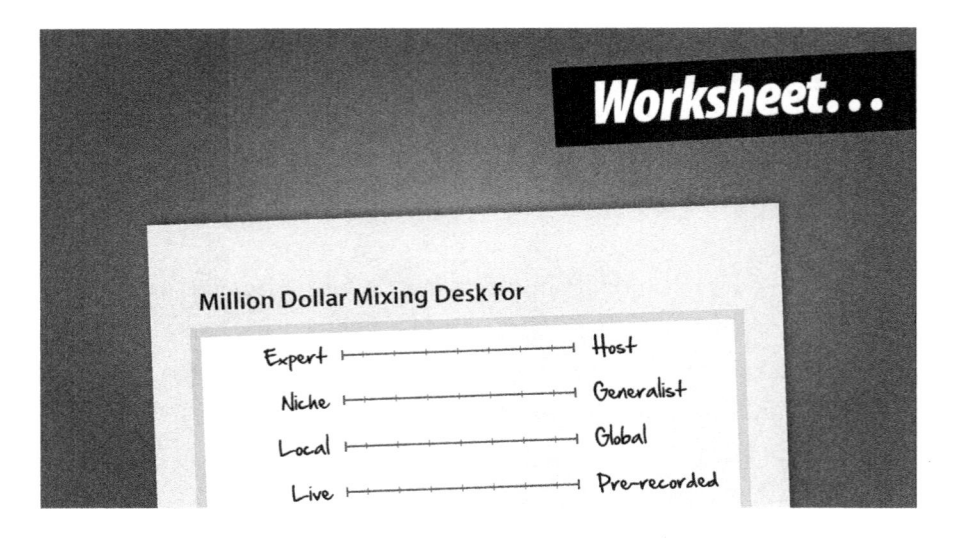

You can download The Million Dollar Mixing Desk from www.MillionDollarCoach.com/kit.

Chapter 8: Unpack IP

In the last chapter, we talked about moving away from traditional one-on-one, time-for-money coaching to something new, something more leveraged. The question is, what are you going to replace your old one-on-one coaching with? What's your new product?

Well, the good news is that your new product's already in your head — there's loads of knowledge and experience in there. We just need a way to get that stuff out of your head and into a box, some kind of package that people can see, understand, and want. And we need a way that's efficient because there's going to be lots of content.

But you don't just need lots of content; you need great content. If you look around your marketplace, you've probably got some competition, and those competitors are offering people the same kind of results that you're offering them. If you can't make your stuff stand out, you're going to drown in a sea of sameness.

So how do you stand out? By making your intellectual property truly unique. Set yourself apart from everybody else by the way your stuff looks, feels, and works.

The way it works is crucially important. When you work one on one with a client, you'll ask them, "What do you need most today?" They tell you their problem, and you reach into your bag of tricks and say, "Okay, you know what, you need *this* ..."

You respond to your client's needs. That's awesome when you've got a one-on-one relationship. There's a place for this kind of responsive coaching when you're working with groups, too. Whether it's one-on-one or with groups, the client's situation is the same: They're looking to you for leadership. They want you to lead them from where they are to where they want to be.

When you package up your knowledge and experience into a product, you're taking the random bag of tricks you've built up over the years, all your knowledge and experience, and you're turning it into a system. You're building a sequence of steps people can follow, one after the other, that leads them to the outcome they need.

When you package up your IP like this, like a product they can buy off the shelf, you make it easy for them to think, "You know what? This sounds exactly like it'll solve my problem. I want it."

We're going to turn your experience into IP, and we're going to use that intellectual property to build and launch lucrative products and programs. Ready?

Why do you want to unpack your IP?

Get some money back in my wallet, so I don't need to be there. To stand out even more. It's not doing any good just sitting in my own head. Easy to buy, easy to deliver. Yes. *I want to stop running myself ragged and trying to be everything to everybody.* John, perfect. *It means you own it and you can leverage it. I've been struggling to create a system that works*, says Jan. Yes, time to step it up. *So much to share, amazing life. It's too time-poor. Get credibility. Get out of my head, serve others. More impact, more freedom.* Alister says, *I've got the garage full, wallet empty problem.* Yeah. *I want a leverage system that runs on autopilot. Help more people, bigger scale, make more money.* Exactly right.

Colin

This is Colin. He lives in Sydney and he's a legend, a super smart cat. We've been working together for a few years now on his Attract, his Convert, and his Deliver. On the delivery side of things, Colin put a $3,000 program together called the "Productivity Academy". It's a short program that helps people learn how to be more productive and effective at work.

Ally

Ally's program is called "Get Your Shit Together". Right? Ally's amazing; she's an incredible woman. She's a psychologist, just full of mojo and personality, and she's got this crazy program. Can you guess what it helps people do?

Todd

Todd's a smart cat, a Canadian guy who moved to New York. He's just launched a great program called the 90-Day Year. Here's the model that underpins the whole thing. It sells for $2,000. Great course. Todd did $550,000 from its launch.

That's what happens when you build this type of products and the marketing engine that fuels them.

Turn Ideas Into Intellectual Property

How do you turn the ideas in your head into valuable intellectual property? First, let me acknowledge a great friend of mine, an incredibly smart guy, Matt Church. Matt's an absolute legend of a guy. He's the one who taught me all of this a few years ago and, frankly, it changed my life. I'm going to give you a mini version now, enough to help you understand what we mean by turning ideas into intellectual property.

Matt taught me the anatomy of an idea. Everything we build, all our content, our courses, our programs, they're all built on ideas, so it's critical that you get a feeling for how they work and how to formulate them effectively.

Ideas exist on three distinct levels. First, there's the concept itself. If anyone's ever said to you, "Get to the point!" they're telling you to state your concept, as clearly and succinctly as you can. The point is the concept; it's a simple statement that encapsulates your idea.

When you make your point, you have to back it up with some evidence, some facts or stories that prove your point is valid, true, or correct. This is where you get down to the details. You'll say, "Let me give you an example," or "Here are the statistics …" or "Let me show you how this worked for Bill."

When it comes to the details, you're going to want two kinds of stuff: left-brain stuff and right-brain stuff. Left-brain stuff is statistics, facts, figures, checklists, and step-by-step processes. Right-brain stuff is stories, anecdotes, and pictures. Make sure you've got at least one of each kind of evidence for every point you make.

After you've made your point and backed it up, you want to take everything up a level and explain how this idea relates to other ideas. You want to put your idea into context, to paint a picture for your audience so they can see how it fits with what they already know.

Again, you'll want some left-brain context and some right-brain context. For left-brain context, we'll draw a model. What's a model? If you spend any time with me, you'll see me draw heaps of these. This book is full of them. They're simple drawings constructed from basic shapes — circles, triangles, or squares — that help explain your point. They help you draw out the fine distinctions and extra dimensions that let your audience connect your point to their knowledge and experience. Left-brain context takes care of the analytical side of things.

For right-brain context, we use a metaphor. We say, "This thing is like that thing." Look at the title picture at the top of this section (which is taken from the slide I use when I present this topic on a webinar or in a live presentation). The metaphor here is that ideas are like steam: You have them, but you can't really see or grab hold of them. If we take the steam and cool it down a bit, we get water. We can see water now, but we still can't grab hold of it. If we cool it down some more, the water turns to ice. It's three dimensional and solid. We can see it, and we can pick it up.

That's what we want to do with your ideas. We want to turn them into something that's three dimensional and solid. We do that with stuff, points, and pictures.

When Matt taught me how to capture ideas like this, he used a 'pink sheet'. A pink sheet is a worksheet designed specifically for capturing the concept behind an idea, the content that backs it up, and the context it relates to. It's divided into three sections: The concept goes in the middle of the page, the context goes up the top, and the content goes down the bottom.

Behind every principle in this book — every principle I've ever taught — there's a pink sheet. For example, this section started with the concept, the key point, 'Turn your ideas into IP'. Those were the words I wrote in the middle of the pink sheet.

Create a Core

When we put a few points together to create a content module, we're creating what I call a 'core': one discrete piece of training. A 60-minute webinar, a presentation, or a chapter of a book, they're all cores.

How do you create a core? Well, once again we're going to lean on the shoulders of giants and adapt a framework. Bernice McCarthy invented this framework years ago for helping primary school teachers create lesson plans that rocked.

Bernice figured out that there are four kinds of learners in the world and that the best way to engage everybody was to build a lesson plan that covered these four different learning styles.

For some people, the big question that drives them is, "Why does this matter?" If you give them details before they understand why the details matter, they won't pay attention because they're not interested.

For others, the big question is, "What's this all about?" They want to know the theory, the mindset, the approach, the philosophy, the history behind something before they can really get into it.

Other people are hands-on learners; they just want to know, "Well, okay, how do I do it?" They want step-by-step instructions.

Bernice called her last step 'What if?', which always seemed a little vague to me. I use 'what next' or 'now' instead. I build all my training around this framework: why, what, how, and now. Why it's important, what to know about it, how to actually do it, and what, specifically, to do next or, even better, what to do right now.

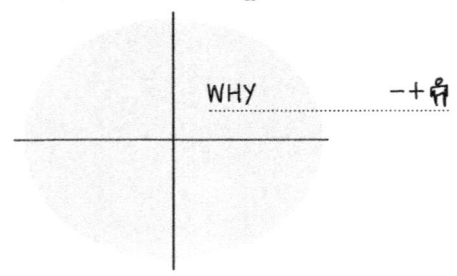

WHY   −+

In the first piece, the 'why' piece, I tap into my target market's fears, frustrations, wants, and aspirations. It goes like this. People are motivated either away from pain or towards pleasure, right? And some of those motivations, their hot buttons, are immediate; they're happening right now. Some of them are imagined: In other words, they could happen in the future.

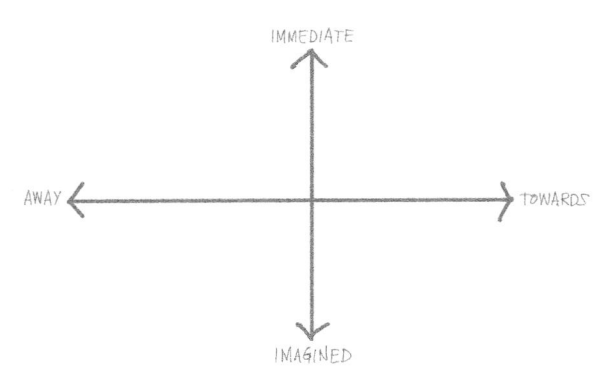

```
                    IMMEDIATE
                        ↑
                        |
        AWAY ←——————————+——————————→ TOWARDS
                        |
                        ↓
                    IMAGINED
```

THE 4 FORCES—FRUSTRATIONS, FEAR, WANTS & INSPIRATIONS.

If we look at that model, we have four different categories to work in. If something's 'away from' right now, that's a frustration. If it's 'away from' in the future, that's something we're scared of in the future; that's a fear. If something's 'towards right now', it's a want. If it's 'towards in the future', it's an aspiration.

All of a sudden we've got a way to talk to the hot buttons that get people moving. One way I get people to take action, whether it's in my marketing, my sales, or my training, is through understanding their fears, frustrations, wants, and aspirations, and feeding them back so clearly that people really get how much I understand their situation.

At the start of every training, talk through these four drivers. When I was building this core about unpacking your IP for you, the fears and frustrations were probably "Yeah, I'm going to replace one-on-one coaching, but what with? It's so slow and hard to create content. I'm going to end up with a garage full of the stuff and no sales." That's the fear. What's the want? You're going to turn your experience into IP, you're going to be able to create world-class content fast and easy, and you're going to launch programs, so that your wallet's full and your garage is empty.

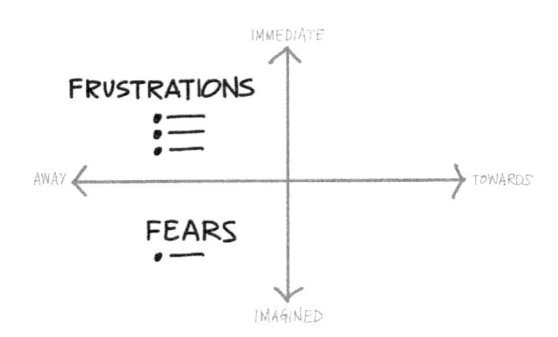

THE 4 FORCES—FRUSTRATIONS, FEAR, WANTS & INSPIRATIONS.

See how it works? The wants and aspirations are easy: They're the positive opposite of the frustrations and fear. You transform a frustration — 'Creating content is time consuming and tedious' — into something they want: 'A method that makes creating content fast and frictionless'.

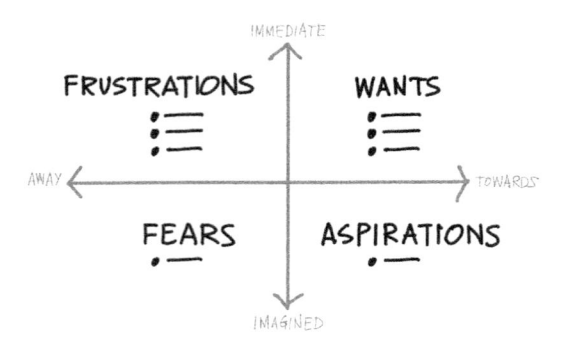

THE 4 FORCES—FRUSTRATIONS, FEAR, WANTS & INSPIRATIONS.

If you're building a presentation, build a *problem stack* with three frustration slides and one fear slide (which takes care of the 'away' side of the model), then build a *promise stack* with three want slides and one aspiration slide (which takes care of the 'towards' side). Add a *proof stack*, placeholder slide for your case study or client story, and there's your why stack done. Then we move onto the 'what' piece.

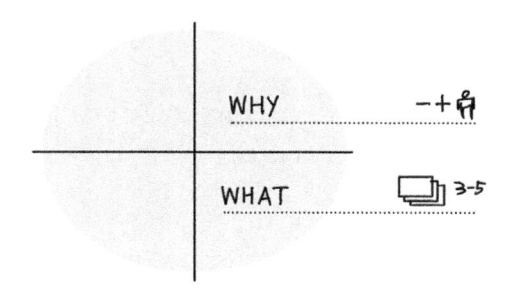

The *what* piece is where you teach your three to five key principles. Each key principle has its own pink sheet.

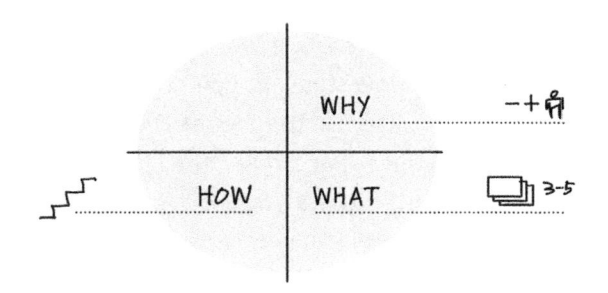

CREATE A CORE-USE A FRAMEWORK FOR BUILDING CONTENT.

In the *how* piece, you'll teach them the step-by-step procedure, how to go about whatever it is you're showing them.

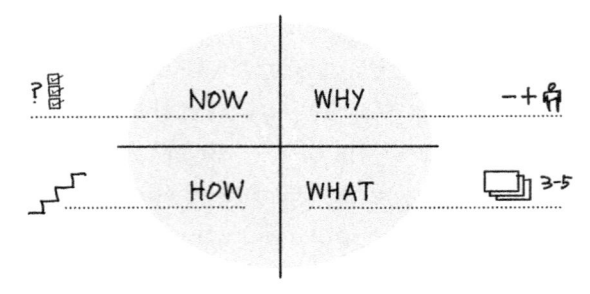

CREATE A CORE-USE A FRAMEWORK FOR BUILDING CONTENT.

In the *now* piece, you lay out their homework, the specific steps they need to do now in order to get started.

> I'm going to open it up now and answer any questions you've got. Then, I'll give you the homework. When I create a core, whether it's for a webinar, a chapter of a book, or a live event, I adapt a little bit depending on each one of those outputs, but it's all built around this core, this why, what, how, now piece. Does that make sense? *Yeah, good, loving it.*
>
> What I do when I create a course, or a webinar, just like I did with you, is explain the concept. I'm now showing you how to do it. Every time I get to one of these black lines on the model, the boundary between *why* and *what*, or between *what* and *how*, that's my opportunity to install an interactive piece, to ask you a question. Every time I cross one of those lines, I check in with you. That's my 'How do I make it rock?' secret. Remember before when we were talking about delivering workshops, not webinars? Well, that's how you do it. Create a core. That's how we build all the modules we're going to need to leverage your delivery; whether it's a short course, or a 12-month program, that's how every module is structured.

Build a Signature System

A signature system is a structured way to move someone from the situation they're in now to the result that they desperately want. It's like a mountain climber looking up a steep, difficult mountain face in the Alps. (Did you spot the metaphor?) Where's the climber right now? He's at basecamp. Where does he want to be? He wants to be at the summit, at the top of the mountain. How's he going to get there? What's the best, safest route to the top? What are the key milestones or landmarks along the way?

A signature system is like a route description for the climber. Start here, go this way, pass these milestones, get to that place. Signature systems make problems easier to understand. They make results easier to achieve, and best of all, they make products easier to sell.

How to Build Your Signature System

Signature systems are built around three components. Number one, what's the core problem your prospects have? What's the problem that needs solving? If you remember those four forces — frustrations, fear, wants, and aspirations — here we're focussing on the frustrations and fear. These are the problems we need to solve.

```
FRUSTRATIONS  |                              | WANTS
─────────────────────────────────────────────────────────
FEAR          |                              | ASPIRATIONS

PROBLEM  ☹                                   ☺ PROMISE
```

YOUR SIGNATURE SYSTEM—6 OR 7 KEY STEPS MOVE PEOPLE FROM PROBLEM TO PROMISE.

Next, what's the promise that you're offering? This is like saying, "Hey, if you're going to work with me, it's going to get awesome. We're going to achieve this, that, and this other thing together." This part's all about their wants, their big aspiration.

So now you know where they are and where they want to go. If you had to get a group of 20 people from here to there quickly, what steps would you take? Lay out the six or seven key steps that move people from the problem to the promise — that's a signature system.

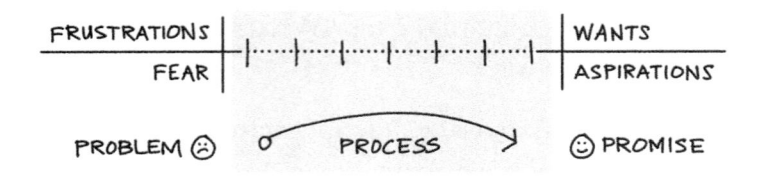

```
FRUSTRATIONS  |—|—|—|—|—|—|  | WANTS
─────────────────────────────────────────────
FEAR                          | ASPIRATIONS

PROBLEM  ☹     PROCESS  →     ☺ PROMISE
```

YOUR SIGNATURE SYSTEM—6 OR 7 KEY STEPS MOVE PEOPLE FROM PROBLEM TO PROMISE.

Let's look at an example so you can see what I mean.

We run a program called Million Dollar Coach Implementation Program to help people scale up to $10,000 per month quickly. If you're just starting out, or you're struggling to hit the $10,000/month mark consistently, you can sign up for the Million Dollar Coach Pilot Program. There's one module a week for nine weeks, and when you're done, you'll have a $100,000 coaching business. It's a little bit epic.

If you look at the structure of that program, you'll see there's a Why video, a What video, three How videos, and a What Next video. That structure looks familiar, right? It's the structure we talked about for building a core.

Then, if you look into any one of those videos, say the Magnet video, you'll see we teach the Why, the What, the How, and the What Next for building killer lead magnets. You can listen to the audio, watch the video, and open up the worksheets for building your own lead magnet and giving it a great name.

In addition to the weekly video, there's a weekly Q&A call so people have a chance to ask any questions they have. That way, we can move them along if they're stuck somewhere.

They're coming; we'd better build it!

The time to start marketing and selling your signature system is right after you've mapped out the problem and your promise, laid out the key steps or modules, and fleshed out the key points for each of them. In other words, you want to sign people into your program before you've actually built any of the pieces you're going to deliver.

Most people think, "I'll build it and they will come." They spend ages and ages building their thing, and they never get around to delivering it, or they end up building something nobody wants. They build it, and nobody comes. Then they've got the 'garage full, wallet empty' problem. You don't want that.

Once you know people are buying what you're selling, start putting your training material together. We delivered the first Million Dollar Coach Implementation Program as a webinar with our first intake of clients, and those recordings became the videos that people watch as part of the online course. We took nine weeks to build the Million Dollar Coach Implementation Program because we built it week by week, together with the clients.

The Signature System

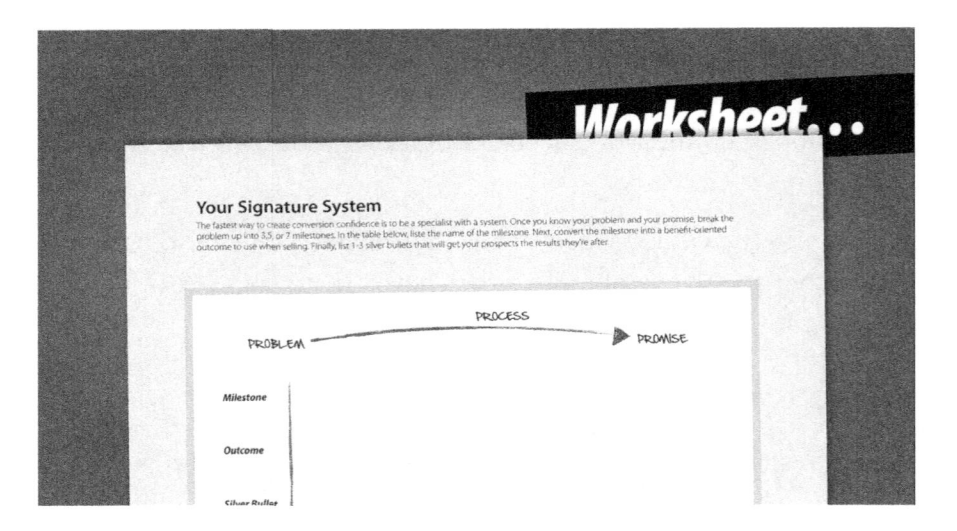

You can download The Signature System worksheet from www.MillionDollarCoach.com/kit.

> What I want to know is, what's been most valuable for you so far about this idea of turning your ideas into IP?
>
> *Systemise everything, all of it! Need to create a six-week course, ASAP.* That's great, you really do. *Pink sheets, learning styles. Never been able to build a signature system, but I can see how to do it*

now. Great! *All mind-blowing. Anatomy of an idea. Beautiful.* Love that. *Concept, context, content.* Love that. *Framework to develop frameworks, genuinely elegant. Effective and simple.* Yes. *Beautiful.*

Louise says, *Unless there's a freaking fire, I'm not going anywhere.* Dion says, *Do you build the video courses in real time? If so, how do you do that?* A little bit like I'm doing with you right now. First, I outline the content. I'm writing a book, so I've got a framework called The Book Builder, and it's one page per chapter. I give the worksheets to the designers, and they build the slides. Then we deliver the session, usually with an audience (like in a webinar), but sometimes it's just me by myself or with my wingman. We record it, then shoot the recording off to the editor who cuts it up into the Why, What, How, and Now sections, and adds in the slides and worksheets. That's basically it. The only time I put in is sketching out the worksheets and doing the delivery; the team takes care of everything else.

Sell it and build it. Yeah, totally, mate. Why build something that you don't even know people want? Sell it first, and then build it as you go. *How long does it take for you to create your program?* Black Belt's a work of art. I've been doing it for five years and I make it better every single month because I'm obsessed, like I'm literally building the world's best system for smart, successful coaches to scale. I'm on a mission. I'm going to be doing this for years.

The Million Dollar Coach Implementation Program is nine weeks long and took eight weeks to build. Took us about 10 minutes to outline it, figure out what the signature system was. It took us about two hours to design the content. It took us an hour and a half per module to record, and then the team did the back-end stuff.

What if you want to do short, but the outcome takes a longer time than eight weeks? Then teach them how to get a smaller outcome in eight weeks.

I'm going to Santa Monica. Will all these tools and such be available there? Yeah, these are all in the workbook at the Million Dollar Coach Intensive. Literally every single worksheet I've showed you is pulled straight out of the Million Dollar Coach Intensive.

How do you decide what to give away for free? This is a great question. How do you decide what to give away for free and what to keep for paid content? Firstly, everybody's terrified about giving away their best stuff, but think about what happens if you don't give away your best stuff. They'll get your stuff that nobody wants anymore, right? They'll be judging you based on your crap stuff. My model is really simple. I give freely of my information, and I earn the right to charge a premium for implementation. Can I just be really blunt with you? Knowing this stuff won't change a damn thing in your business. You can be on this webinar with me, even if you took a hundred pages of notes. Nothing is going to change until you implement. I guarantee, you'll get stuck implementing and the only way to get the result you want fast is to have a guide. Somebody to help you through the process.

I give freely of the knowledge, and I charge a premium for implementation. Just understand, information and implementation, two completely different things.

All right. I'm going to show you how to do this because you're going to need some help. I think, just so you know, I reckon there are two kinds of people you need with you on this journey.

You need heads, and you need hands. Heads give you strategy. Strategy, direction, coaching, yeah? Hands help you with implementation, they help you do the stuff. This has been my strategy for years. I pay a premium for heads who give me the knowledge and skill, and I save on hands.

Cheaping-out on the strategy part or the head part is the biggest false economy ever. It seems like you're saving money, but it's costing you millions of dollars in lost opportunities. That's what we're going to talk about next: how to get hands for your business.

Chapter 9: Leverage Talent

This book is all about transition. It's moving from Coaching Business 1.0 — from your old, one-on-one, manual business — to new ways of attracting leads, new ways of converting those leads into clients, and new ways to deliver your services. It's about transitioning to Coaching Business 2.0.

Any transition is kind of messy. While you're in this transition phase, there are heaps of demands on you. Lots of jobs to do. Existing clients to keep happy, new stuff to build. New technology to get your head around, all while you're hunting for new business and keeping the money coming in.

The big problem right now is that you're the bottleneck.

You're at the centre of the three main processes in your business — attracting, converting, and delivering — so scaling up just becomes really hard work. It's like you're grinding away and there's all this friction.

We've got to remove the bottleneck — we've got to remove you from the daily grind — and we've got to eliminate the friction. Your business needs some lube to keep the wheels spinning freely and everything flowing smoothly.

Here's what happens when you're not in the middle of everything, doing everything, all of the time. You get to play to your strengths; you get to do the stuff that you're uniquely gifted and amazing at. You get to do the stuff that gives you energy, and avoid the stuff that drains the life out of you.

Creating leverage through virtual assistants, by using technology effectively and with little hacks, makes a huge difference to your day. It gives you the space you need to make the transition work.

> Here's what I want to know: Why do you need a virtual assistant or a virtual team?
>
> Dion called it, *Lube. I knew it.* Why do you need it? I'll give you 10 seconds right now to type it into the chat box. *I need to go from ideas to implementation.* Yeah, to kick ass faster. I hate the technology totally. *To save my remaining hair,* says Bill. That's funny. Nat, love that. *Because sometimes it's just too boring. I'm already tired of how it is. I can't imagine having to do more.*

Remember, the key to this business model is less. *Teamwork makes the dream work.* Yeah. *To keep me on track. I can make more money per hour than I can pay a VA by miles.* Right? Let's say you have a great virtual assistant, like someone amazing. A thousand dollars a month, full-time, 40 hours a week, completely dedicated to you to get all your needs done. A thousand dollars. Tell me you can't, in the 20 hours that it saves you, tell me you can't make 10, 20 thousand dollars, right? Of course you can.

Carl

I want to introduce you to a client, Carl, who's also on my team. Carl's an automation genius. He's one of the guys I go to when I need an automated campaign. A while ago now, Carl was doing project work for people, and he was the bottleneck in his business. He couldn't scale because it was just him. He was booked out three months in advance, but he had no way and no capacity to go faster.

What did he do? Carl assembled a team of ninjas to help him deliver the work. ('Ninjas' is our affectionate term for our Filipino virtual assistants, also sometimes known as 'ninja-pinos'. More on them in a moment.)

Having the team take care of tech work means Carl is free to focus on strategy. He templated all the work, and now his business handles 50-100 clients instead of just a few. Because he freed himself up dramatically, Carl's business is on a massive growth trajectory.

Find the Magic, Dump the Trash

Look at all the tasks that you do in your business. I bet you do some high-value, high-dollar, high-passion activities, the kind of work you do when you're in front of an audience, or teaching a webinar, or working directly with clients. It's the kind of high-dollar, high-value magic only you can do.

Then there's everything else, all the day-to-day stuff that isn't your genius at all, but it has to get done. Dan Sullivan talks about four levels of activity (based on Martin Broadwell's original idea).

First, there are things that, frankly, you can't do at all, where you're just incompetent. You hate doing those things, and you usually mess them up.

> What's one thing you're incompetent at?
>
> *Technology stuff, quality control, tech, finance, details, graphic development, paperwork.* Right. All kinds of incompetence right there.

Then there are jobs you're okay at. You're not great at them, you find them hard work, they're a bit of a drag, and — at best — you turn out OK work.

> What's an example of that? Something that you're competent at? *Tech, admin, report-writing. Heaps of people saying tech. Marketing, copywriting.* Right. *Writing, speaking, crafting ideas.* Okay. There's incompetent, there's competent, and then there's excellent.

One step up from competent, there's work you excel at, where you have a superior skill. People notice you're really good at it, but you know your skill is learned, not natural. This kind of work usually doesn't give you energy, and you don't really love it.

> What's an example of something you're great at because you had to be? *Bookkeeping, admin, doing the tax, design, paid marketing, connecting, admin.* Right. *Public speaking.* You're good at that, but you don't love it. That's excellent.

Then there's the fourth category. Dan calls it *unique ability*; I call it your genius. It's the stuff you're incredible at. People talk about it.

They notice you have this spooky talent. You didn't have to learn it; you were born that way. You've been doing it since you're a kid. It gives you energy. You find it's so effortless, so easy, you almost don't recognise or value it yourself as something special. You find it endlessly fascinating, and you could do it forever. This stuff is the magic.

> What's something that fits in that bucket for you? *Product creation, being in front of people live, idea generation, speaking, inspiring and selling, coaching, networking, drinking coffee, training, inspiring others, writing.* Right.

Here's the thing: There's the magic, and everything else is the trash, including the work you're competent at, and even the work you excel at. We want to build you a business where you only work the magic and where you can dump the trash.

Install Kung Fu

If you're going to dump the trash — offload these tasks to somebody else — you'll need to train them up fast. We want to install Kung Fu like Neo and Morpheus in the movie *The Matrix* when they plug that cable into the back of Neo's head and Morpheus says, "Tank, load the fight program." Neo blinks for a few moments, and when he opens his eyes, he says, "I know Kung Fu."

That's how we want to train our team. Plug in a cable and upload all the information our team needs to do the job. In Black Belt, we use a tool called *The 5-Minute Freedom Finder* to help with this, but you could just as easily record yourself doing the task with a tool like Jing and share the recording with your assistant. (Another option is hiring an assistant who already knows what to do. We'll get to that in a moment.)

When I first started out, my goal was to claw back 30 minutes of extra free time each week. I started with one virtual assistant in the Philippines. We have a team of five full-time virtual assistants now taking care of all the day-to-day jobs in the business, and I have loads of free time to do what I do best.

Because I run a coaching business, and my clients are all coaches, they started asking me, "How can I get a team like yours?" Well, these days it's simple. One of my assistants started a company to provide virtual assistant (VA) services for my clients, the same way he provides them for me. We're affiliated with them, of course, but we don't own their business. Obviously, we have a vested interest in their success, so I visit the Philippines twice a year to train them up on our systems and tools. At the last count there were 113 VAs working with our Black Belt clients. Why does it work so well? Because those VAs all come with the Kung Fu pre-installed.

Build an Onramp

You know when you're joining a freeway or a motorway, there's an onramp, right? The onramp's job is to get you from the slow, low-speed, suburban streets up to freeway speed so by the time you're merging with freeway traffic, you're not holding people up. You're in the flow.

That's what we want to do for your virtual assistants: build them an onramp so they can go from zero to hero in about six weeks. Here's the process our Black Belt clients use to get new VAs up to speed. There are three main phases — relationship, rhythm, and rollout. Each one takes about two weeks.

Relationship is all about getting the relationship off on the right foot, working out how you work best, how they work best, how you communicate, and what their role is.

Rhythm is about them taking up the internal rhythms of your business, getting familiar with your calendar, understanding the things that happen daily, weekly, monthly, and establishing contact with your customers.

Rollout is where they start taking over your marketing, where they start being responsible for bringing leads into your world.

Here's how it breaks down, week by week:

RELATIONSHIP | ROLE / CONNECTION

BUILD AN ONRAMP-GET YOUR TEAM UP TO SPEED FAST.

In week one, the focus is on connection. You get to know them; they get to know you. They learn about you, your products and services, your clients, your goals, your vision for the business. They get set up with all the technology. We work through a tool we call The Communication Builder, which helps you work out the best ways to work together. For example, how do you prefer to receive information? How do you prefer to give it? That sort of thing.

In week two, the focus is on their role. What's their specific job? You do your activity inventory, listing out all the daily, weekly, monthly, and quarterly tasks. You filter them by frequency, then by genius, excellence, competence, and incompetence, and you give them all the tasks they're going to take over, identifying the first five for them to systemise.

Now we're into the rhythm phase.

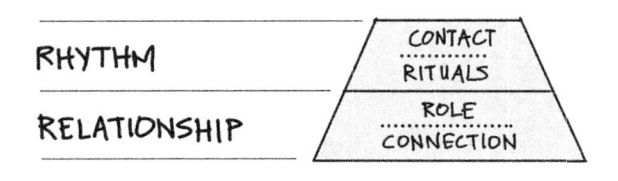

RHYTHM | CONTACT / RITUALS
RELATIONSHIP | ROLE / CONNECTION

BUILD AN ONRAMP-GET YOUR TEAM UP TO SPEED FAST.

Week three is about rituals. They take over your calendar, if you want them to. They start managing your daily, weekly, and monthly meeting schedule. If you're a control freak and don't like to be managed, that's cool, but I can use all the managing I can get. I'm the last person who should be in charge of my calendar.

Week four is about contact. Now they're starting to manage your email inbox and your contact with clients. They're handling your prospects one on one. In our business, we worked out that there are 16 specific emails we send all the time. Some are sales, some are client management, some are membership related, technical stuff like account details, credit cards, and so on. They all have templates now, and the VA takes over all that routine work.

The next phase, rollout, is about marketing.

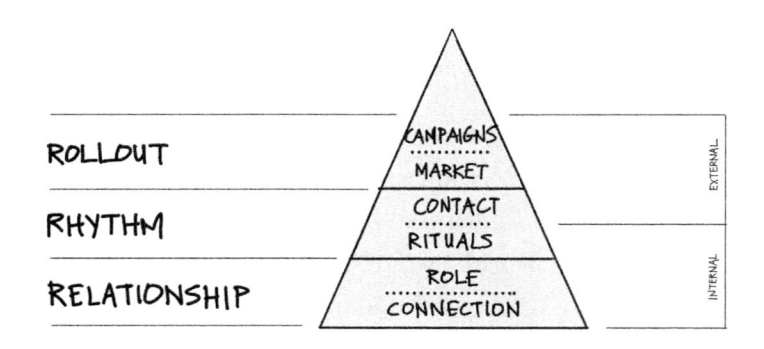

BUILD AN ONRAMP-GET YOUR TEAM UP TO SPEED FAST.

In week five, they send their first email broadcast to your database. There's a system for this, of course (there's a system for everything in Black Belt). We use a worksheet called The Email Builder to map out what you want to say. You voice record the copy, then they transcribe it, edit it, and show it to you. After you okay everything, they broadcast the email, and after it's all done you review all the steps together. Eventually, they can manage the whole campaign from start to finish. You map the campaign out at the start, they run the whole thing, and you debrief together at the end.

If we look at this, there are two things going on here. The first three weeks are internally focused, right? They're all about you, and them, and your internal business processes. The last three weeks are external; they're market-facing, messaging clients and prospects, broadcasting and managing campaigns.

In six weeks, we get them right up to highway speed.

The Virtual Assistant Onramp

Here's how to build your onramp.

First, do your activity inventory. List all the tasks you currently do. What are your daily, weekly, monthly, and quarterly jobs? Just list them out. What do you do marketing-wise, sales-wise, admin-wise? What do you do with clients? What do you have to do technology-wise? What do you have to do with accounts and finance? List them all out.

Step two, filter them by frequency. Sort them into daily, weekly, monthly, quarterly, yearly, and other. We're going to systemise dailies and weeklies first because they happen more often, and you'll get more bang for your systemising buck.

Step three, rank your tasks by incompetence, competence, excellence, and genius. Circle anything that's daily or weekly, and below your pay grade — that means anything you've ranked as 'incompetent' and probably most of the things you've ranked as 'competent' too. Now, identify the top five tasks you've circled and hand them off to your new VA.

Worksheet...

Title	1 CONNECTION	2 ROLE	3 RITUAL	4 CONTACT	5 MARKET	6 CAMPAIGN
	Relationship			Rythm		Rollout
The Virtual Assistant On-Ramp						
Outcome	Get to know each other, your business & goals	Create daily, weekly, monthly, quarterly task lists.	Establish internal communication rhythm.	VA can manage your inbox, calendar & 1:1 communication.	VA sets up, cleans up CRM; Sends broadcast.	Roll out first full campaign.
Coach	Prep for meeting	Activity Inventory	Default diary	Review & tweak email templates.	Select/share CRM, Record broadcast with voxer	Decide on campaign
Team	Get to know you meeting	Review & prioritise tasks to systemise	Schedule D: check-in W: tactical M: strategic Q: plan	Review emails & language palette	Review & send broadcast	Brief on campaign. Review: #wins #next
VA	Set up tools i.e.: email, buffer, gcal, voxer, slack, dropbox	Project plan and Systemise	Timetrade, Systems.	Load emails as canned replies, manage inbox Systems.	Import/clean list Send broadcast. Systems.	Set up campaign Systems.

We use a tool to help us upskill our VAs quickly, which is called The Virtual Assistant Onramp. By the way, the six-week VA onramp is a course that we built for our clients, just like we talked about in Signature Systems. It's actually two programs that run simultaneously. There's the six-week course the coach goes through, and there's the six-week course that the virtual assistant goes through. The VA goes through the program a week before you do, so when you ask them to do stuff, they know exactly what has to happen, and they feel really comfortable and confident about doing it.

You can download The VA Onramp from www.MillionDollarCoach.com/kit.

> What I want to know is, what was most helpful for you about working with a virtual assistant? What'd you learn? What'd you notice? What would you like to share?
>
> *Mind-blown. The worst part is that the stuff is below my pay grade and I'm incompetent at it all.* Mate, that's the best part. Obvious tap

on the shoulder, Kenneth, to get rid of that stuff. *The onramp. The onboarding was most valuable, yeah, the six-week onramp.* By the way, there's a workbook and videos for the coach, and videos for the VA. It's pretty slick. I love it. *System step by step, four steps. Six-week, onramp. Hire on attitude, build up skills.* Ian reckons I'd systemise getting systemised. I totally would, there's a framework for everything. I reckon you're a dozen frameworks away from a million dollar business, mate. The secret is, how do you get the frameworks and how do you install them into your business as quickly as you can? *Yeah, really impressed with this onramp system. Everyone says get a VA, and then it's just a shitload of work from there.* Totally. Mark says, *Great as always. Seriously thinking about attending live MDCI.* If this is killer, imagine what would happen if we had two days together to actually work on this stuff in your business. Right? It would be freaking amazing. You should totally come to MDCI. I'm going to post it in for you, Mark. Right now, you should go there immediately, mate, and sign yourself up.

Summary: The Million Dollar Path

We started this book by talking about a leveraged coaching model. We said there are three things you need to do. You need to attract, you need to convert, and you need to deliver. The way we're taught to attract is manual marketing, knocking on doors, cold calling, collecting cards, following up, and chasing.

The way we're taught to sell on the convert side of things is one on one; it's slow, hard work. You have to deal with objections, excuses, and stalls. You spend hours chasing prospects. Maybe they sign off as a client; often they don't.

Then, when you do finally sign up a client, on the delivery side of things, you lock yourself into time-for-money coaching. More hard manual work.

All those activities are built around your time and your effort. And guess what? You don't have an infinite supply of either of those things. There are only so many hours in a day, and you've only got so much energy you can expend before you get tired, exhausted, and burned out.

In the first section of the book, we talked about how to attract in an automated way, how to use online lead generation to bring you the clients you need, and how to warm them up to the point where they're an 8, 9, or 10 in terms of how likely they are to buy from you, to give you money.

In the second section, on the Convert side of things, we talked about moving from the old way of selling one on one to the new way of selling with webinars and live events.

And in the third section, on Delivery, we talked about the transition from time-for-money coaching to something much more leveraged where you can help more people, have more fun, and make more money. We talked about unpacking your intellectual property, and building it into a signature system people can buy and get results with. We talked about leveraging the talents of others to get stuff done.

This model is the key; it's your pathway from being stuck to bumping yourself up quickly and becoming a million dollar coach.

We broke down the nine strategies, the nine projects that turned my one-man show into a million dollar coaching business. You can do the same thing too. What I'm going to do next is walk you through the Black Belt business plan. It's the plan I used — and still use — to grow my business, and it's the same plan I use with all my Black Belt clients. It'll help you take everything we learned so far and apply it in your world.

Here are three things you need to know before we get started.

Plan For Action

Here are two kinds of plan you can create as a coach or consultant right now. You can create a strategic plan or a street plan. Strategic plans are long, boring documents you write for a bank or an investor when you want a loan. Almost nobody reads them after they're written, and they usually sit on a shelf collecting dust. Strategic plans are of no practical use for you and me. We need to be fast and agile. We don't want a strategic plan at all. We want a street plan.

A street plan isn't a big-picture plan; it's not full of what-ifs, SWOT analyses, or risk assessments. It's a very practical *what-do-I-do-this-week* plan. It's a *how-do-I-turn-this-into-money-right-now* plan.

Street plans tension just the right amount of big-picture vision with concrete, right-now, today actions. There's no point doing too much planning because, as the Prussian general Baron von Moltke once said, "No campaign plan survives the first point of contact with the enemy." Or, as the American philosopher, Mike Tyson, put it, "Everyone has a plan until they get punched in the face."

Instead of setting a plan in stone forever, we want a simple plan that gives you direction and tells you exactly what to do today, right now, this minute.

Call a 20

When I was a teenager, I loved NBA basketball. American basketball was fast and athletic; it was death-defying and full of action. One of the things that was different about American NBA basketball compared with the basketball we played here in Australia was a timeout called a '20', and any player could call one.

It wasn't like a full timeout; they didn't sit down to brainstorm and strategise. Those 20 seconds are a quick little huddle to figure out, "Right, here's what we're going to do. Ready? Let's go." They're just long enough to pause the madness, to figure out our next actions, and put them into play.

Enter the 3 Atmospheres

I heard a great marketer say the best business people in the world think in three distinct time zones, and that's what sets them apart from everybody else. They think about three years, three months, and today, right now. In a moment, we're going to create a street plan that works through these three zones. Where do you want to be in three years? What are our projects for the next three months? What do we need to work on today?

The Black Belt Business Plan

We use a system called the Project Runway, and the tool we use is The Black Belt Business Plan. You can download a copy from www.MillionDollarCoach.com/kit. Or you can just grab a blank sheet of paper and divide it into four quadrants.

Worksheet...

VISION
30,000 ft | 3 YEARS

THE BLACK BELT BUSINESS PLAN—A STREET PLAN FOR ACTION.

We're going to start up in the top left quadrant, where it says 30,000 feet, 3 years, vision. Imagine we're in a plane, flying up at 30,000 feet where you can see clearly, all around, for miles and miles. Where do you want to be in three years' time? What do you want your business to look like in three years? How do you want things to be different? How do you want your revenues, your personal income to be different?

190   MILLION DOLLAR COACH   Taki Moore

Write that down in the top left box. Seriously, I mean it. Start writing now. Just bullet points, first thing that comes to mind. Write them down.

How do you want your clients to be different? How do you want the number of clients to be different? Love that. What about your products and your programs? Are you still one-on-one-ing? Or are you way more leveraged in three years' time? How do you want your products to be different? How do you want your reputation in the marketplace to be different? How do you want to be known by your clients, in the industry, by colleagues? What do your weeks look like? Are they free, or are they full up?

How do you want your year to look different? If you zoom out and look at a full-year view of your calendar, how do you want that to look? Where are the holidays blocked out? Are there lots of free days, or is it all work with no escape?

Where do you want to be living? Me, I want to live in the summer, wherever it's hot, that's where you'll find me, with my laptop coaching people all around the world. Where do you want to be? Who do you want to have with you? Who's on the team now who wasn't there earlier? Is there a virtual assistant or a virtual team freeing you up?

Lastly, if you think about all these things and all you've come through to get to this place, how does it feel? I want you to write down three words to describe how it feels to have that business three years from now.

Awesome, you're doing great. Let's just pause and check in.

Have a look at the list you've got there in the top left quadrant, the 30,000-foot, three-year vision. How does that feel? Is it good? Are we doing well? We're on the right track. If we did those things, your world would be epic, right?

> Do me a favour: Write down how that would feel. Give me three words that describe how you'd feel. *It'll be life-changing, motivating, effing awesome. I'll be free. Un-effing believable. Peaceful, awesome, relieved, free, fun, fantastic.* Great. We know we're on the right track.

Let's look at the top, right-hand side. We've thought about the three years and vision, now let's bring it down a little bit. We're thinking about 20 thousand feet, 12 months, and goals. Here's what comes next. We've just painted a picture; we've created a vision for our next three years. What we're going to do next is start to land the plane. We're going to bring our altitude down to 20,000 feet; we're going to look at the next year.

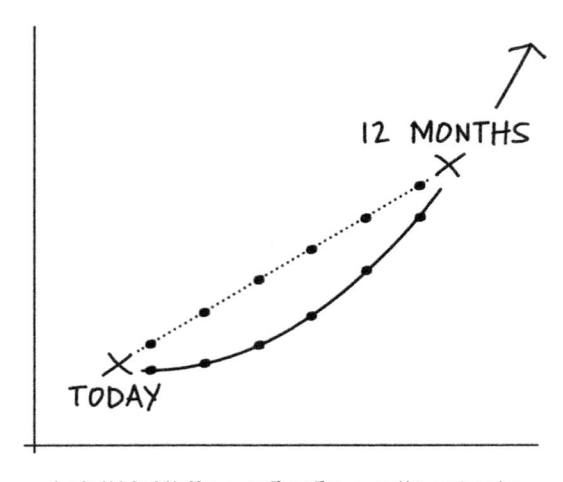

COACHING BUSINESS 2.0–AUTOMATED, 1: MANY, LEVERAGED

Now, most people, when they're breaking down their goals, draw a straight line between where they are now and where they want to go, and they just assume that everything's going to pan out evenly. Have you ever noticed that things don't work out like that? You usually take a while to ramp up, right? We're going to cut ourselves some slack and assume there's a bit of a ramp-up phase.

VISION 30,000 ft | 3 YEARS	**GOALS** 29,000 ft | 12 MONTHS

THE BLACK BELT BUSINESS PLAN—A STREET PLAN FOR ACTION.

In the top right box, write down where you think you'd need to be on your ramp-up curve in a year's time. Where would you need to be in a year to be completely on track in three years?

Look at everything you've got in the left box and write down the one-year version of it in the right box. Make each one very tactical, very measurable. The question is, "How much, by when?" The when's decided, it's one year, so you just have to decide how much. You want to look at your list in a year's time and check each box. Did I achieve that, or didn't I?

VISION 30,000 ft | 3 YEARS	**GOALS** 29,000 ft | 12 MONTHS
PROJECTS 10,000 ft | 90 DAYS	

THE BLACK BELT BUSINESS PLAN—A STREET PLAN FOR ACTION.

MILLION DOLLAR COACH   Taki Moore

Now we're going to zoom down here to the bottom left. We're not thinking about the three-year, 30-thousand-foot vision, or the 12-month, 20-thousand-foot goals. Our new time frame is 90 days. We're not thinking about vision or goals anymore; we're thinking about projects.

The question is this: "If that's where I want to be in 12 months' time, what are the three projects I need to get done in the next 90 days to be completely on track?"

Remember, we're choosing these projects to keep us on track for our 12-month goals. If your business is just you working on your own, maybe with a VA, then three projects is enough. If you have a team to back you up, you can work on more projects at once. We do three marketing projects and three program projects every quarter, but keep in mind I've got a team of virtual assistants helping me.

What three projects are going to move you closer to your 12-month goals? Before you start to write them down, let me give you a quick tip about naming your projects: Start them with a verb. Something like, "Map out a signature system" or "launch a webinar", yeah? ("Join Black Belt" is a great project name, just by the way.)

What are the three projects you need to do in the next 90 days? Write those down right now.

VISION 30,000 ft | 3 YEARS	**GOALS** 29,000 ft | 12 MONTHS
PROJECTS 10,000 ft | 90 DAYS	**ACTIONS** RUNWAY | 1 WEEK

THE BLACK BELT BUSINESS PLAN—A STREET PLAN FOR ACTION.

Okay, we're down to the last step. Here's what we do. This piece of paper is going to be super valuable for you. Now, if you've got some Post-it notes handy, grab one and stick it over this box. If you don't have a Post-it note, just write in the box for now, then get yourself a Post-it note for next week.

So far we've talked about three years, 12 months, and 90 days; we've talked about vision, goals, and projects. Our new timeframe is one week, and we're talking about the specific actions you need to take to move your projects forward.

Every single week, I stick a new Post-it note on top of last week's note. I never pull the old Post-it notes off; I just stick the new one over the top. The question I ask is, "If those are my 90-day projects, what three actions do I need to take this week to move me forward?"

Let's say you've got three projects over there on the left. You can choose one action for each project, or you can go, "You know what, I'm just going to focus all three actions on this one project and really move things along."

Either way is completely fine, whichever works best for you at the time. The question is, what are the one, two, three actions you need to take in the next seven days to move yourself forward? Again, start your actions with a verb. And I suggest making one of them really easy, something you can do in less than two minutes, anything super simple that gets you moving forward.

When you complete your three actions each week, you're on track with your 90-day projects. If you complete your 90-day projects, you'll be on track with your 12-month goals. If you hit your 12-month goals, you'll be completely on track for your three-year vision.

Focus on your three actions for this week, and the rest takes care of itself. Every week, on Monday morning, we stick a new Post-it note over last week's actions. We call it *Post-it Monday*. On *Finished It Friday* we share, "Here's what I finished this week".

If you'd like to go deeper on these nine strategies or projects, then the fourth action should be "sign up for Million Dollar Coach Intensive". If you want to have me walk you through it, then come to the LIVE Million Dollar Coach Intensive. We hold this six times a year. If you're interested, the URL is www.MillionDollarCoachIntensive.com

If you can't make it to the live event, but you're serious about growing, we should talk about Million Dollar Coach Implementation Program that gets you to $10K a month.

If you want to scale, and if you're over $10K a month, the fourth thing I'm going to get you to do is think about whether we can help you in the Black Belt program. Here is the link: www.joinblackbelt.com/session

You'll complete a two-minute questionnaire which gets you onto the calendar for a call. In ten minutes, we'll have a quick chat to determine if we can help you or not. With the pre-session questionnaire, and then on the call, we'll be able to say, "Mate, here's what's possible for you." We'll help you identify what's the one thing that is bothering you the most right now and give you three specific things to work on quickly. That's what we do in the launch and scale audit.

That's your fourth action. If you want to go deeper with the nine strategies, then come to the Million Dollar Coach Intensive at www.MillionDollarCoachIntensive.com

Two questions come up often: "What are the differences between Million Dollar Coach Intensive and the Million Dollar Coach Implementation Program?" The Million Dollar Coach Intensive is a two-day workshop designed to go deep into the stuff that you've been learning here. We spend two days and go deep into these nine strategies. You get a 192-page workbook, with lots of exercises that we do together, and you walk out of there clear about what to do next.

The Million Dollar Coach Implementation Program is the perfect system if you know that you're not at $10,000 a month yet, and you want to get there quickly. It's an eight-week program, which gets you super clear on who to serve and what to say to them. Also, what's the offer you need to create? We build out your product, your signature system, design it live so you can have a conversation with people, and have them say, "Wow, that sounds awesome," and give you money.

In week three, we build a lead magnet that will get people to give you their email address. We go deep on your Facebook ads and drive traffic to the lead page. We'll build a thank you page that has people booking for a triage call with you. We teach you how to do the triage call in detail. We'll have a strategy session in detail, and you will get clients. The Million Dollar Coach Intensive live training is the learn-it-in-depth strategy, the whole system. Exactly as we've been doing, but deep. The Million Dollar Coach Pilot Program is when you think, "Great, love it. Learning stuff is cool, but I want to get to $10K in the next eight weeks." Then choose the Pilot Program.

The next question is: "Should I go straight to Black Belt and forget the Pilot Program?" Mate, if you're not doing $10,000 a month yet, we won't let you join Black Belt. It's as simple as that. We built the Pilot Program to get people ready. By the way, that plan that we just went through, you have my full permission to teach that to clients; just give me credit and say you have it from your friend, Taki Moore. It's a helpful way to get people really clear.

What's going to make the difference to you and your coaching business, is doing the strategies and implementing.

> "A good plan, violently executed right now, is better than a perfect plan next week."
> — George S. Patton

George Patton, an American General — famous for riding on the front of a tank across the desert, pistols in his hands, to go shoot Hitler personally — was an execute-and-implement guy if ever there was one. "A good plan, violently executed right now, is better than the perfect plan next week."

If you've been following me for a while, you may wonder, "I attended Million Dollar Coach Intensive a few years ago. Has the content changed?" It has definitely evolved, but here's the question I have for you. If you attended a few years ago, did you do anything with it? We just had an amazing lady who was at the very first live US event I ever did. It was in this tiny little room in Santa Monica. Then I met her recently in San Francisco. She said, "I came to this two years ago, but I didn't do anything with it."

I said, "Well, how did your business change?"

"It didn't."

"Right. What's going to be different this time?"

She's changed, and now she's doing amazing work.

I'd love to meet you sometime at a live workshop or in a program. Please, spread the word about this book and the website, www.MillionDollarCoach.com/book with your friends. If there's anything I can ever do, please let me know.

Thanks so much for being part of my world, and I wish you every success for the future.

Printed in Great Britain
by Amazon